P9-DVD-026

Carnegie Commission on Higher Education
Sponsored Research Studies

WHERE COLLEGES ARE AND WHO ATTENDS:
EFFECTS OF ACCESSIBILITY ON COLLEGE
ATTENDANCE
*C. Arnold Anderson, Mary Jean Bowman, and
Vincent Tinto*

NEW DIRECTIONS IN LEGAL EDUCATION
*Herbert L. Packer and Thomas Ehrlich
abridged and unabridged editions*

THE UNIVERSITY AS AN ORGANIZATION
James A. Perkins (ed.)

THE EMERGING TECHNOLOGY:
INSTRUCTIONAL USES OF THE COMPUTER
IN HIGHER EDUCATION
Roger E. Levien

A STATISTICAL PORTRAIT OF HIGHER
EDUCATION
Seymour E. Harris

THE HOME OF SCIENCE:
THE ROLE OF THE UNIVERSITY
Dael Wolfle

EDUCATION AND EVANGELISM:
A PROFILE OF PROTESTANT COLLEGES
C. Robert Pace

PROFESSIONAL EDUCATION:
SOME NEW DIRECTIONS
Edgar H. Schein

THE NONPROFIT RESEARCH INSTITUTE:
ITS ORIGIN, OPERATION, PROBLEMS, AND
PROSPECTS
Harold Orlans

THE INVISIBLE COLLEGES:
A PROFILE OF SMALL, PRIVATE COLLEGES
WITH LIMITED RESOURCES
Alexander W. Astin and Calvin B. T. Lee

AMERICAN HIGHER EDUCATION:
DIRECTIONS OLD AND NEW
Joseph Ben-David

A DEGREE AND WHAT ELSE?
CORRELATES AND CONSEQUENCES OF A
COLLEGE EDUCATION
*Stephen B. Withey, Jo Anne Coble, Gerald
Gurin, John P. Robinson, Burkhard Strumpel,
Elizabeth Keogh Taylor, and Arthur C. Wolfe*

THE MULTICAMPUS UNIVERSITY:
A STUDY OF ACADEMIC GOVERNANCE
Eugene C. Lee and Frank M. Bowen

INSTITUTIONS IN TRANSITION:
A PROFILE OF CHANGE IN HIGHER
EDUCATION
(INCORPORATING THE 1970 STATISTICAL
REPORT)
Harold L. Hodgkinson

EFFICIENCY IN LIBERAL EDUCATION:
A STUDY OF COMPARATIVE INSTRUCTIONAL
COSTS FOR DIFFERENT WAYS OF ORGANIZ-
ING TEACHING-LEARNING IN A LIBERAL
ARTS COLLEGE
Howard R. Bowen and Gordon K. Douglass

CREDIT FOR COLLEGE:
PUBLIC POLICY FOR STUDENT LOANS
Robert W. Hartman

MODELS AND MAVERICKS:
A PROFILE OF PRIVATE LIBERAL ARTS
COLLEGES
Morris T. Keeton

BETWEEN TWO WORLDS:
A PROFILE OF NEGRO HIGHER EDUCATION
Frank Bowles and Frank A. DeCosta

BREAKING THE ACCESS BARRIERS:
A PROFILE OF TWO-YEAR COLLEGES
Leland L. Medsker and Dale Tillery

ANY PERSON, ANY STUDY:
AN ESSAY ON HIGHER EDUCATION IN THE
UNITED STATES
Eric Ashby

THE NEW DEPRESSION IN HIGHER
EDUCATION:
A STUDY OF FINANCIAL CONDITIONS AT 41
COLLEGES AND UNIVERSITIES
Earl F. Cheit

FINANCING MEDICAL EDUCATION:
AN ANALYSIS OF ALTERNATIVE POLICIES
AND MECHANISMS
Rashi Fein and Gerald I. Weber

HIGHER EDUCATION IN NINE COUNTRIES:
A COMPARATIVE STUDY OF COLLEGES AND
UNIVERSITIES ABROAD
*Barbara B. Burn, Philip G. Altbach, Clark Kerr,
and James A. Perkins*

BRIDGES TO UNDERSTANDING:
INTERNATIONAL PROGRAMS OF AMERICAN
COLLEGES AND UNIVERSITIES
Irwin T. Sanders and Jennifer C. Ward

GRADUATE AND PROFESSIONAL EDUCATION,
1980:
A SURVEY OF INSTITUTIONAL PLANS
Lewis B. Mayhew

THE AMERICAN COLLEGE AND AMERICAN
CULTURE:
SOCIALIZATION AS A FUNCTION OF HIGHER
EDUCATION
Oscar Handlin and Mary F. Handlin

RECENT ALUMNI AND HIGHER EDUCATION:
A SURVEY OF COLLEGE GRADUATES
Joe L. Spaeth and Andrew M. Greeley

CHANGE IN EDUCATIONAL POLICY:
SELF-STUDIES IN SELECTED COLLEGES AND
UNIVERSITIES
Dwight R. Ladd

STATE OFFICIALS AND HIGHER EDUCATION:
A SURVEY OF THE OPINIONS AND
EXPECTATIONS OF POLICY MAKERS IN NINE
STATES
Heinz Eulau and Harold Quinley

ACADEMIC DEGREE STRUCTURES,
INNOVATIVE APPROACHES:
PRINCIPLES OF REFORM IN DEGREE
STRUCTURES IN THE UNITED STATES
Stephen H. Spurr

COLLEGES OF THE FORGOTTEN AMERICANS:
A PROFILE OF STATE COLLEGES AND
REGIONAL UNIVERSITIES
E. Alden Dunham

FROM BACKWATER TO MAINSTREAM:
A PROFILE OF CATHOLIC HIGHER
EDUCATION
Andrew M. Greeley

THE ECONOMICS OF THE MAJOR PRIVATE
UNIVERSITIES
William G. Bowen
(Out of print, but available from University Microfilms.)

THE FINANCE OF HIGHER EDUCATION
Howard R. Bowen
(Out of print, but available from University Microfilms.)

ALTERNATIVE METHODS OF FEDERAL
FUNDING FOR HIGHER EDUCATION
Ron Wolk
(Out of print, but available from University Microfilms.)

INVENTORY OF CURRENT RESEARCH ON
HIGHER EDUCATION 1968
Dale M. Heckman and Warren Bryan Martin
(Out of print, but available from University Microfilms.)

*The following technical reports are available from the Carnegie Commission on Higher Education, 2150 Shattuck
Ave., Berkeley, California 94704.*

RESOURCE USE IN HIGHER EDUCATION:
TRENDS IN OUTPUT AND INPUTS, 1930–1967
June O'Neill

TRENDS AND PROJECTIONS OF PHYSICIANS
IN THE UNITED STATES 1967–2002
Mark S. Blumberg

The following reprints are available from the Carnegie Commission on Higher Education, 2150 Shattuck Ave., Berkeley, California 94704.

ACCELERATED PROGRAMS OF MEDICAL EDUCATION, by Mark S. Blumberg, reprinted from JOURNAL OF MEDICAL EDUCATION, vol. 46, no. 8, August 1971.*

SCIENTIFIC MANPOWER FOR 1970–1985, by Allan M. Cartter, reprinted from SCIENCE, vol. 172, no. 3979, pp. 132–140, April 9, 1971.

A NEW METHOD OF MEASURING STATES' HIGHER EDUCATION BURDEN, by Neil Timm, reprinted from THE JOURNAL OF HIGHER EDUCATION, vol. 42, no. 1, pp. 27–33, January 1971.*

REGENT WATCHING, by Earl F. Cheit, reprinted from AGB REPORTS, vol. 13, no. 6, pp. 4–13, March 1971.*

COLLEGE GENERATIONS—FROM THE 1930S TO THE 1960S, by Seymour M. Lipset and Everett C. Ladd, Jr., reprinted from THE PUBLIC INTEREST, no. 25, Summer 1971.

*The Commission's stock of this reprint has been exhausted.

AMERICAN SOCIAL SCIENTISTS AND THE GROWTH OF CAMPUS POLITICAL ACTIVISM IN THE 1960S, *by Everett C. Ladd, Jr., and Seymour M. Lipset, reprinted from* SOCIAL SCIENCES INFORMATION, *vol. 10, no. 2, April 1971.*

THE POLITICS OF AMERICAN POLITICAL SCIENTISTS, *by Everett C. Ladd, Jr., and Seymour M. Lipset, reprinted from* PS, *vol. 4, no. 2, Spring 1971.**

THE DIVIDED PROFESSORIATE, *by Seymour M. Lipset and Everett C. Ladd, Jr., reprinted from* CHANGE, *vol. 3, no. 3, pp. 54–60, May 1971.**

JEWISH ACADEMICS IN THE UNITED STATES: THEIR ACHIEVEMENTS, CULTURE AND POLITICS, *by Seymour M. Lipset and Everett C. Ladd, Jr., reprinted from* AMERICAN JEWISH YEAR BOOK, *1971.*

THE UNHOLY ALLIANCE AGAINST THE CAMPUS, *by Kenneth Keniston and Michael Lerner, reprinted from* NEW YORK TIMES MAGAZINE, *November 8, 1970.*

PRECARIOUS PROFESSORS: NEW PATTERNS OF REPRESENTATION, *by Joseph W. Garbarino, reprinted from* INDUSTRIAL RELATIONS, *vol. 10, no. 1, February 1971.**

. . . AND WHAT PROFESSORS THINK: ABOUT STUDENT PROTEST AND MANNERS, MORALS, POLITICS, AND CHAOS ON THE CAMPUS, *by Seymour Martin Lipset and Everett C. Ladd, Jr., reprinted from* PSYCHOLOGY TODAY, *November 1970.**

DEMAND AND SUPPLY IN U.S. HIGHER EDUCATION: A PROGRESS REPORT, *by Roy Radner and Leonard S. Miller, reprinted from* AMERICAN ECONOMIC REVIEW, *May 1970.**

RESOURCES FOR HIGHER EDUCATION: AN ECONOMIST'S VIEW, *by Theodore W. Schultz, reprinted from* JOURNAL OF POLITICAL ECONOMY, *vol. 76, no. 3, University of Chicago, May/June 1968.**

INDUSTRIAL RELATIONS AND UNIVERSITY RELATIONS, *by Clark Kerr, reprinted from* PROCEEDINGS OF THE 21ST ANNUAL WINTER MEETING OF THE INDUSTRIAL RELATIONS RESEARCH ASSOCIATION, *pp. 15–25.**

NEW CHALLENGES TO THE COLLEGE AND UNIVERSITY, *by Clark Kerr, reprinted from Kermit Gordon (ed.),* AGENDA FOR THE NATION, *The Brookings Institution, Washington, D.C., 1968.**

PRESIDENTIAL DISCONTENT, *by Clark Kerr, reprinted from David C. Nichols (ed.),* PERSPECTIVES ON CAMPUS TENSIONS: PAPERS PREPARED FOR THE SPECIAL COMMITTEE ON CAMPUS TENSIONS, *American Council on Education, Washington, D.C., September 1970.**

STUDENT PROTEST—AN INSTITUTIONAL AND NATIONAL PROFILE, *by Harold Hodgkinson, reprinted from* THE RECORD, *vol. 71, no. 4, May 1970.**

The Commission's stock of this reprint has been exhausted.

WHAT'S BUGGING THE STUDENTS?, by Kenneth Keniston, reprinted from EDUCATIONAL RECORD, American Council on Education, Washington, D.C., Spring 1970.*

THE POLITICS OF ACADEMIA, by Seymour Martin Lipset, reprinted from David C. Nichols (ed.), PERSPECTIVES ON CAMPUS TENSIONS: PAPERS PREPARED FOR THE SPECIAL COMMITTEE ON CAMPUS TENSIONS, American Council on Education, Washington, D.C., September 1970.*

INTERNATIONAL PROGRAMS OF U.S. COLLEGES AND UNIVERSITIES: PRIORITIES FOR THE SEVENTIES, by James A. Perkins, reprinted by permission of the International Council for Educational Development, Occasional Paper no. 1, July 1971.

FACULTY UNIONISM: FROM THEORY TO PRACTICE, by Joseph W. Garbarino, reprinted from INDUSTRIAL RELATIONS, vol. 11, no. 1, pp. 1–17, February 1972.

MORE FOR LESS: HIGHER EDUCATION'S NEW PRIORITY, by Virginia B. Smith, reprinted from UNIVERSAL HIGHER EDUCATION: COSTS AND BENEFITS, American Council on Education, Washington, D.C., 1971.

ACADEMIA AND POLITICS IN AMERICA, by Seymour M. Lipset, reprinted from Thomas I. Nossiter (ed.), IMAGINATION AND PRECISION IN THE SOCIAL SCIENCES, pp. 211–289, Faber and Faber, London, 1972.

POLITICS OF ACADEMIC NATURAL SCIENTISTS AND ENGINEERS, by Everett C. Ladd, Jr., and Seymour M. Lipset, reprinted from SCIENCE, vol. 176, no. 4039, pp. 1091–1100, June 9, 1972.

THE INTELLECTUAL AS CRITIC AND REBEL, WITH SPECIAL REFERENCE TO THE UNITED STATES AND THE SOVIET UNION, by Seymour M. Lipset and Richard B. Dobson, reprinted from DAEDALUS, vol. 101, no. 3, pp. 137–198, Summer 1972.

THE POLITICS OF AMERICAN SOCIOLOGISTS, by Seymour M. Lipset and Everett C. Ladd, Jr., reprinted from THE AMERICAN JOURNAL OF SOCIOLOGY, vol. 78, no. 1, July 1972.

THE DISTRIBUTION OF ACADEMIC TENURE IN AMERICAN HIGHER EDUCATION, by Martin Trow, reprinted from THE TENURE DEBATE, Bardwell Smith (ed.), Jossey-Bass, San Francisco, 1972.

THE NATURE AND ORIGINS OF THE CARNEGIE COMMISSION ON HIGHER EDUCATION, by Alan Pifer, based on a speech delivered to the Pennsylvania Association of Colleges and Universities, Oct. 16, 1972, reprinted by permission of the Carnegie Foundation for the Advancement of Teaching.

*The Commission's stock of this reprint has been exhausted.

COMING OF MIDDLE AGE IN HIGHER EDUCATION, by Earl F. Cheit, address delivered to American Association of State Colleges and Universities and National Association of State Universities and Land-Grant Colleges, Nov. 13, 1972.

MEASURING FACULTY UNIONISM: QUANTITY AND QUALITY, by Bill Aussieker and J. W. Garbarino, reprinted from INDUSTRIAL RELATIONS, vol. 12, no. 2, May 1973.

PROBLEMS IN THE TRANSITION FROM ELITE TO MASS HIGHER EDUCATION, by Martin Trow, paper prepared for a conference on mass higher education sponsored by the Organization for Economic Co-operation and Development, June 1973.

*American
Learned Societies
in Transition*

American Learned Societies in Transition

THE IMPACT OF DISSENT AND RECESSION

by *Harland G. Bloland*

Associate Professor of Higher Education
Teachers College, Columbia University

and *Sue M. Bloland*

Graduate Student in Sociology
New School for Social Research

A Report Prepared for
The Carnegie Commission on Higher Education

MCGRAW–HILL BOOK COMPANY

New York   St. Louis   San Francisco   Düsseldorf

London   Sydney   Toronto   Mexico   Panama

Johannesburg   Kuala Lumpur   Montreal

New Delhi   São Paulo   Singapore

*The Carnegie Commission on Higher Education,
2150 Shattuck Avenue, Berkeley, California 94704,
has sponsored preparation of this report as part
of a continuing effort to obtain and present
significant information for public discussion.
The views expressed are those of the authors.*

AMERICAN LEARNED SOCIETIES IN TRANSITION
The Impact of Dissent and Recession

This book was set in Palatino by B. Handelman Associates, Inc.
It was printed and bound by The Maple Press Company. The
designers were Elliot Epstein and Edward Butler. The editors
were Nancy Tressel and Janine Parson for McGraw-Hill Book
Company and Verne A. Stadtman and Karen Seriguchi for The
Carnegie Commission on Higher Education. The index was prepared
by Audre Hanneman. Milton J. Heiberg supervised the production.

Library of Congress Cataloging in Publication

Bloland, Harland G
American learned societies in transition: the
impact of dissent and recession.

"Prepared for the Carnegie Commission on Higher
Education."
Bibliography: p.
1.   United States—Learned institutions and soci-
eties.   I.   Bloland, Sue M., joint author.   II.   Car-
negie Commission on Higher Education.   III.   Title.
AS25.B57   061'.3   74-1339
ISBN 0-07-010107-8

123456789MAMM7987654

Contents

Foreword

Student and faculty unrest on American college and university campuses was never greater than in the 1960s and early 1970s. At the same time, a related branch of the American intellectual "family"—the learned societies—faced similar pressures from newly formed, internal radical caucuses. This was perhaps inevitable. For these collegial associations of researchers, practitioners, and teachers of the scientific and humanities disciplines draw their leadership and the majority of their membership from the academic world. And, like colleges and universities, the American learned societies have been deeply affected by the changing values and commitments of society and of their members.

In their analysis of these changing values and the conflicts they have engendered within the learned societies, Harland and Sue Bloland have given us a rare perspective of the forces for change in a major segment of the academic profession. We are grateful for their thoughtful account of a period when ideologies, politics, and personalities often veiled the events and their significance in a heady confusion.

Clark Kerr
Chairman
Carnegie Commission
on Higher Education

June 1974

Acknowledgments

We would like to express our gratitude to Richard Colvard, Trent Schroyer, and Vincent Tinto for their very helpful comments on portions of this manuscript, and to Karen Seriguchi and Verne Stadtman for their valuable editorial contributions to the final draft. We are also deeply indebted to the many persons who gave so generously of their time and insight in the interviews which informed this study.

*American
Learned Societies
in Transition*

1. Introduction

Since the latter part of the 1960s, American learned societies have been under assault from a variety of groups who have viewed these associations as agencies through which to reform values and practices in the disciplinary professions. The assault was first launched in 1967 and 1968 by left activists and intellectuals who organized as caucuses within a wide range of learned societies to challenge the positivist tradition in American scholarship and the elitist governance structure of these disciplinary associations that have guarded this tradition. Their efforts to mobilize their associations as agencies of change in the academic reward system were quickly joined by women and members of minority groups who demanded recognition and support from learned societies in their quest for equal (and in some cases compensatory) opportunity in the disciplines. And finally, with the onslaught of the academic recession, the claims of these reformers were followed by demands from job seekers that learned societies assist them in the search for employment and take an active role in alleviating the job crisis for Ph.D.'s by exerting influence upon the employment policies and practices of organizations (most importantly, the academic institutions) that house the disciplines.

The following is primarily an account of dissident activity within American learned societies in the years between 1967 and 1972 and of the organizational response to new claims made upon these associations by the various caucuses and interest groups within them. We begin by tracing the general pattern of membership growth and expansion of activities in the post-World War II period through which the small, narrowly focused scholarly societies of the late nineteenth and early twentieth centuries assumed a somewhat more instrumental, or "professional," character, emerging as a major locus of influence on the internal affairs of the academic disciplines and, in some cases, representing these professions in their expanding relations with external institutions and groups. It was the central role played by learned societies in the postwar development of the disciplinary professions that suggested their strategic importance to activists in the late 1960s as organizations through which to effect change in the reward and opportunity structures in these disciplines.

We next examine the nature of the reform activity initiated in learned societies in 1967 and 1968 in a general discussion of the types of participants in that activity and in a presentation of three case studies of associations that found themselves challenged from within. The three associations—the American Political Science Association, the Modern Language Association of America, and the American Physical Society—represent, respectively, a social science, a humanistic discipline (or, in this case, a composite of several disciplines), and a natural science. While no group of three organizations could be considered "typical" of the total (highly diverse) population of American learned societies, the case studies presented here do serve to illustrate some recurrent themes in the organizational and disciplinary critiques articulated by various dissident groups within scholarly associations as well as some common patterns of organizational response to reform activity. At the same time, these three studies suggest some general differences in character among major associations representing the social sciences, those representing the humanities, and those representing the natural sciences and point to some significant divergences in the radical critiques of the organizations in these three spheres.

Only two or three years after the emergence of radical and minority-group caucuses in American disciplinary associations, the academic recession and a resulting shortage of jobs for Ph.D.'s had begun to take precedence over earlier reform issues as the most immediate preoccupation of many learned-society members and of society leadership in most of the disciplines. While the early stages of the recession had immediate repercussions within these associations in the form of member demands for assistance with the employment crisis, the long-range impact of academic retrenchment on the character and role of learned societies promises to be more profound than even these early manifestations suggest. A discussion of the trend toward faculty unionization in the 1970s and of its implications for the future of American disciplinary associations concludes our report.

2. The Traditional Function and Character of American Learned Societies

The origin and development of learned societies is closely linked with the emergence of the modern university in American society. Both organizations took root during the last two decades of the nineteenth century and the early years of the twentieth century, reflecting a new academic commitment in the United States to the advancement of knowledge through scholarly research. The founding fathers of American learned societies were, for the most part, faculty members at American universities, and these societies have continued into the 1970s to be dominated by their academic members—from among whom association leadership is largely drawn, and toward whose needs and interests learned-society activities are most directly geared—despite the growing number and proportion of nonacademicians who have recently joined their ranks.

Created primarily for the purpose of advancing and disseminating knowledge within the academic disciplines, American learned societies have played a critical role in developing, standardizing, and formalizing the disciplines as theoretical and methodological structures, in promoting the establishment of emerging subfields of knowledge as independent spheres of study, and in supporting these subfields in the intrauniversity competition for status and institutional resources. At the same time, learned societies contributed to the "professionalization" of the disciplines, drawing scholarly identification and loyalty away from institutions of academic employment toward the national disciplinary peer group and promoting the growth of national reward or career systems within each of the disciplines. They also served as convenient loci for the operation of a national academic labor market.

DIFFERENCES BETWEEN ACADEMIC AND PROFESSIONAL ASSOCIATIONS

As the academic disciplines assumed an increasingly professional character (see Jencks & Riesman, 1968), however, the university professor differed strikingly from such traditional models of the professional as the doctor and lawyer, and his disciplinary associations have differed significantly from professional associations as exemplified by the American Medical Association or the American Bar Association.

For the disciplines, as well as for medicine and law, the development of training and research programs within the university was a necessary step in the process of occupational professionalization. For medicine and law, however, institutionalization within the university followed an earlier stage of practice and was accompanied by a continued emphasis on practice as the most characteristic activity of these professions. For the academic disciplines [whose "primary structural anchorage," in Parsons' (1966, p. 125) words, "is clearly in the academic world"], establishment in the university meant a gradual withdrawal from practical pursuits and a striking deemphasis on the intellectual responsibility of the scholar toward the uses of his product in the practical sphere or toward service to specific clientele groups in the society. In the academic disciplines and in the scholarly associations within which these disciplines were nationally housed, a narrow commitment to scholarship—to the advancement of knowledge for its own sake—reflected a pervasive assumption that the advancement of knowledge was ultimately of benefit to mankind in general and to the society in which it took place in particular and that "an inherent power for order in the world would absorb [the scholar's] product into its beneficent economy without his assuming responsibility for the process" (Schorske, 1968, p. 980). Thus, the reward structure in the academic disciplines and their associations lent meager support to dedication to or accomplishment in the application of scholarly knowledge—despite continuous agitation from some subgroups within the associations to grant these activities a more central place in the professional role of the academician and in the affairs of scholarly societies.

At the same time, learned societies did not, as a rule, accept a fiduciary role in the professional activities of their members. While professional associations assumed responsibility at the turn of the century for developing and enforcing codes of professional ethics for their practicing members—designed to protect the client of the private practitioner and to prevent the imposition upon the profession of regulation by some outside agency—most learned societies did not develop such codes. Their memberships were made up predominantly of scholars whose work was carried on within the university and whose professional autonomy within that context relied much more heavily upon scholarly expertise than upon a claim to a strong service orientation to "clients"—in this case, college and university students. One important reason why a deemphasis on a service orientation could prevail in the academic disciplines was that ultimate responsibility for the welfare of students lay with the university itself. Students are formally the clients of the university as an institution rather than of individual professors, and matters related to their well-being have not generally preoccupied the professional bodies to which professors belong.

Neither did learned societies assume responsibility for establishing and maintaining formal standards of professional training and performance. Since the primary work of the academic scholar (research and publication) is essentially public in nature, it is readily available for assessment both by colleagues within the university and by members of the wider disciplinary community and (unlike much of the professional work of the private practitioner) is continuously subject to colleague control (although this control is exercised primarily through the distribution of rewards within the discipline rather than through direct forms of punishment or ostracism). As a result, the maintenance of reasonably uniform national standards of performance requires no formal machinery within the academic disciplines for the certification of members or for the accreditation of graduate training programs, although such formal machinery is characteristic of professional associations. Standards of professional training, about which there has come to be widespread informal agreement within the disciplines, are enforced in university departments through formalized degree requirements. It is the university that officially "certifies" those who complete its advanced disciplinary programs, on the recommendation of its graduate departments. At the same time, because academic professionals have controlled the employment policies affecting their colleagues in the university department, standards of scholarly competence have been enforced through the decisions of local professional groups regarding the hiring and promotion of fellow faculty members, tenure, and so on.

Like their counterparts in the applied professions, however, professors did feel the need to create central machinery early in this century to protect favorable conditions of work in the large organizations that employed them. Professional associations were pressed to provide such machinery when urban and industrial conditions threatened the status that practitioner professionals had earlier enjoyed in the rural society of nineteenth-century America. As an increasing proportion of their practice began to be carried on within large corporate structures, doctors and lawyers organized to defend their work autonomy against the imposition of working conditions (including the setting of their fees) by these organizations (Gilb, 1966, p. 35).

Professors, for their part, were alarmed by the processes of bureaucratization that had accompanied the rapid growth of institutions of higher learning. As a result of the university's new size and organizational complexity, it was, they felt, coming under increasing administrative domination. At the same time, the new wealth and visibility of the university seemed to make it more vulnerable than ever to attack from external pressure groups. In the face of these pressures, professors felt the need to organize to defend academic freedom from both internal and external threat and to secure faculty rights and tenure as occupational conditions essential to the conduct of scholarly work. They did not, however, turn to their young learned societies to fight for them on this front. The American Association of University Professors was established in 1915 to serve the common occupational needs of American professors as employees of educational institutions. Focusing its attention upon university policy in relation to academic freedom and tenure, and (more recently) upon salary schedules and collective bargaining, the AAUP has diverted pressure from American learned societies (at least until the early 1970s) to concern themselves with the conditions of academic work.

In contrast to professional associations, then, learned societies had very limited instrumental functions prior to World War II and little organizational machinery for promoting the needs or interests of their members in the university or in the larger society. There have been exceptions to this generalization among the scientific learned societies; for example, the American Chemical Society and the American Institute of Physics have included among their basic concerns the advancement of applied science and have actively promoted the employment of scientists in industry from as early as the 1930s (Barton, 1956, p. 58). For the most part, however, learned societies contributed to the prestige and work autonomy of their members as scholar-professionals through their inward focus on strengthening the claims and enhancing the university status of the disciplines themselves. Even among those few learned societies that included in their constitutions an explicit commitment to improve the occupational position of their members (as did, for example, the Modern Language Association), the tendency in the early part of the century was to pursue this goal by making the field itself "worthy of respect" (Fisher, 1969, p. 21).

ASSOCIATION GOVERNANCE PRIOR TO WORLD WAR II

Engaged in few instrumental activities and having meager assets and relatively small memberships prior to World War II (few of these organizations had as many as 5,000 members before 1940), learned societies operated with fairly simple governance structures and procedures. Despite their formally democratic character, governance patterns in learned societies strongly reflected both the research-oriented reward structure of the disciplines and the institutionally prescribed criteria for evaluating scholarly achievement.

Held to be among the highest honorific awards within the organized national disciplines, learned-society officerships (including positions on key governing bodies) were allocated almost solely on the basis of scholarly accomplishment. And as long as learned societies remained small and relatively uncomplex organizations that were conceived of ideally as homogeneous "communities of scholars," few other organizational or political criteria competed with scholastic or scientific eminence as a basis for the selection of association officers. Under these circumstances, it was considered inappropriate for candidates to compete with each other in public election for association office. Within an academic discipline, assessments of the relative merits of individual scholarship are not arrived at democratically but emerge, rather, out of the operation of the principle of "authority"—out of a consensus of opinion among those members of a discipline deemed most competent to judge the validity and importance of new knowledge (Zuckerman, 1970, p. 241). This principle of authority, which predominates in the allocation of rewards in the disciplines generally, has also predominated in the allocation of officerships (and other honorific rewards) in American learned societies.

Thus, a nominating committee, composed of eminent scholars, typically proposed one candidate for each vacant office who was routinely ratified by an annual "election" (involving a mail ballot or a vote at the annual business meeting) in which a consistently low proportion of association members participated. The choice of the nominating committee was rarely contested, although in most cases, constitutional procedures were available for nominating alternative candidates by member petition.

Elected officials generally served for a one-year term (part-time and unpaid) in a largely honorific capacity. They relied heavily on the greater continuity of service and the organizational abilities of an executive secretary, who played a key role in all organizational decision making. Greater authority generally resided in an association council (whose members served in longer, overlapping terms) that characteristically met only once a year to consider an agenda of society business prepared by the administrative officer. The authority of the council was shared, in varying degrees, with the annual business meeting of the association, which was held in conjunction with annual society meetings and which provided an opportunity for the membership at large to participate in the formal governance of their association. Prior to the late 1960s, however, the annual business meeting in most disciplinary associations was attended almost exclusively by association officers and council members themselves (where a quorum of association members was required for formal decision making, that quorum was achieved only with great difficulty), and so it is not surprising that council decisions were generally ratified by this assembly.

THE
POSTWAR
PERIOD
Most learned societies continued well into the post-World War II period to be characterized by a strong focus on the advancement of knowledge, by a deemphasis upon social responsibility or client relations as a central feature of the disciplinary professions, and by a strong adherence to the merit system in the disciplines as a basis upon which to allocate association leadership positions. This scholarly ethos prevailed despite the tremendous growth and expansion of the disciplines and of their associations following World War II and in spite of profound

changes that began to occur in the relationships between many learned societies and other institutions in society.

Growth and Diversification A number of factors contributed to the accelerated growth and diversification of the academic disciplines—and of disciplinary associations—in the period following World War II. Student attendance at institutions of higher education had been climbing steadily since the 1920s, with a consequent expansion of college and university faculties. (The teaching staffs of American colleges and universities grew from 56,000 in 1922 to 82,000 in 1930, and to over 500,000 by the end of 1970—"Historical Perspectives...," 1971, p. 10.) In addition, the contribution of academic scientists and scholars to the national defense effort during World War II had dramatized the value of research as a national resource and had stimulated substantial government and foundation support of academic training and research programs, first in the natural sciences, and eventually in the social sciences and humanities as well.

A widespread pattern of government and foundation grants and federal contracts developed to support such research-related activities as publication, the translation of foreign journals, visiting-scientist programs, special research conferences, and summer institutes. In some instances (the Modern Language Association, the Mathematical Association of America, and the American Mathematical Society are prime examples), federal support, supplemented by foundation grants, for the development of teaching programs had a major influence in directing subsequent association attention toward the improvement of collegiate and precollegiate instruction. More typically, however, federal and foundation monies contributed to the expansion of association programs related to basic research in the natural and social sciences.

The resulting flurry of scholarly activity gave rise to new subfields of knowledge, new university departments to house them, and new learned societies to promote their growth and independence from related scholarly pursuits. An accelerated production of Ph.D.'s swelled the ranks of the disciplines and learned societies (see Table 1), bringing to an end, for many of these organizations, an era of informal face-to-face gatherings among small, homogeneous groups of scholars.

Many learned societies, in reaction to the increase in doctoral

TABLE 1
Growth of membership in nine learned societies

	1940	1950	1960	1970
American Political Science Association[a]	2,857†	5,126	7,000	18,006
American Sociological Association[b]	1,008	3,241	6,822	13,600
American Anthropological Association[c]	732	2,951	3,951	7,000
American Psychological Association[d]	2,739	7,272	18,215	30,839
Modern Language Association[e]	4,379	6,480	11,610	33,440
American Historical Association[f]	3,573	5,772	9,370	18,000
American Physical Society[g]	3,751	9,472	18,570‡	28,555
American Chemical Society[h]	25,414	63,349	92,193	114,323
American Association for the Advancement of Science[i]	21,067	46,775	57,432	133,364

*The three learned societies that are the focus of Chapters 4, 5, and 6.

† Figure is for 1941.

‡ Figure is for 1962.

SOURCES:

[a] *American Political Science Review* (1941; 1951). Figure for 1960 from *Scientific and Technical Societies of the United States and Canada* (1961). Figure for 1970 obtained from APSA national office, April 1971.

[b] *American Sociological Review* (1940; 1950; 1960). Figure for 1970 obtained from ASA national office, April 1971.

[c] *American Anthropologist* (1941; 1951). Figure for 1960 from *Scientific and Technical Societies of the United States and Canada* (1961). Figure for 1970 obtained from AAA national office, June 1973.

[d] Figures obtained from APA national office, June 1973.

[e] *Publication of the Modern Language Association* (1960; 1970a; 1970b).

[f] American Historical Association (1940; 1950; 1960). Figure for 1970 obtained from AHA national office, April 1971.

[g] Figures obtained from APS national office, April 1971.

[h] Figures obtained from ACS national office, June 1973.

[i] Figures obtained from AAAS national office, April 1971.

degree holders during the 1940s and 1950s, restricted full association membership by limiting voting rights and eligibility for elective office to members with Ph.D.'s or other evidence of professional stature. This restriction was an attempt to defend their research orientation from the potentially less scholarly concerns of their "noncertified" members and to distinguish for the public between qualified scholars and interested laymen. (Nevertheless, non-Ph.D.'s continued to constitute a majority of learned-society members, and their dues remained a critical source of association income.)

Learned societies also responded to the new size and heterogeneity of their memberships by establishing subject-matter sections or divisions within their ranks to accommodate the diverse research specialties of their members. Regional subdivisions of the national organizations, as well as affiliate societies with special subject-matter concerns, also multiplied as learned-society members frequently found in them a closer sense of colleagueship than their national disciplinary associations could continue to provide.

LEARNED-SOCIETY INFLUENCE WITHIN THE NATIONALIZING DISCIPLINES

As the nation's Ph.D.'s were drawn in increasing numbers to posts outside the foremost graduate universities, the disciplinary professions came to include teachers from a greater range of academic institutions, as well as a growing number of research scholars from government and industry. As a result, a more elaborate stratification emerged within the disciplines, with national prestige remaining concentrated among a relatively small proportion of university departments and scholars at the top of the status hierarchy and with a widening gap between the narrow top of that hierarchy and its expanding bottom.

Within this increasingly stratified system, many learned societies came to play an important role in the establishment of standards and the distribution of prestige and, consequently, to wield influence on the development and operations of university departments, on the careers of academic scholars, and, in some instances (most notably, in the social sciences), on the actual direction in the theoretical and methodological development of the disciplines themselves.

With new Ph.D. programs sprouting up in academic institutions of all types and with no formal machinery available for assessing the adequacy of the training they offered (aside from the general accreditation to which their parent institutions were subject), learned-society leadership was pressed to take an active interest in evaluating and improving graduate training in the disciplines. To this end, they appointed committees to concern themselves with curriculum development and the establishment of standards of training and, in a few instances, to make public their own lists of "approved" graduate departments. Generally, however, learned societies have lacked both the necessary organizational resources and a clear mandate from their members to undertake formal accreditation procedures.[1] Rather, it became common practice for emerging college and university departments to look to disciplinary associations for informal assistance with the development of new degree programs or with the assessment of continuing programs (although this was less true for the major graduate schools in the United States than for the more numerous, less prestigious institutions that had begun to offer graduate degrees).

And as the disciplines became increasingly national in orientation, so that more and more careers in these professions came to depend upon the achievement of national status, associations began to play a critical role in the allocation of professional resources—research opportunities, job opportunities, and more importantly, national prestige—among members of their academic discipline. To present a paper at the annual association meeting, to publish in a major association journal, to receive an association fellowship or award, or to be appointed to an organizational post or committee, significantly enhanced the professional status of academic scholars, particularly in a national career system in which rampant growth and specialization had reduced the extent to which scholars could rely on direct familiarity with each other's work as a basis for making professional assessments. Under these circumstances, the learned society became a particularly important national context for the assessment of scholarly work and the distribution of widely visible symbolic rewards.

As a result, where there was a consistent theoretical, methodological, or ideological commitment or bias (however implicit)

---

[1] A committee of the American Historical Association undertook, in 1969, to establish criteria by which graduate departments of history could be evaluated by the profession. Descriptions of Ph.D. programs—submitted to the committee, upon request, by graduate departments themselves—were reviewed and evaluated, and recommendations were made for the improvement of those programs deemed inadequate in one respect or another. The project was abandoned a year later, however, when the association was threatened with legal action by several departments dissatisfied with the evaluation procedure. Apprehensive that the association might be sued under the Sherman Act, AHA leadership chose not to become embroiled in a legal battle over the accreditation issue.

on the part of association editorial boards, program committees, or nominating committees, this preference had the inevitable effect of attracting scholars toward work in the officially "approved" areas, where they were most likely to receive general acceptance and recognition. In this respect, learned-society leadership has sometimes played a critical role in guiding or inhibiting change in the dominant paradigms for research in the disciplines. A particularly strong illustration of association impact on the development of a field is provided by the American Political Science Association in its promotion of the behavioral approach to the study of politics in the 1950s.

RELATIONS WITH THE FEDERAL GOVERNMENT
During the late 1950s and early 1960s, a few learned societies also encountered new pressures to adopt some of the functions that professional associations had performed for their own members since the turn of the century in their relations with external institutions and groups: that is, to serve as vehicles for the promotion and defense of disciplinary interests to the federal government and, at the same time, to assume responsibility for establishing and maintaining standards of ethical conduct for their members as they became increasingly involved with clients outside the university. In these respects, associations representing the social sciences were far more deeply affected than were the natural science or humanistic societies by the changing relationships between their members and government, particularly during the early 1960s.

World War II marked the beginning of a major trend in the United States toward the utilization of academic research to solve technological and social problems related to national defense and domestic affairs. The growing appreciation in industry, and particularly in government, of the practical value of natural and, later, of social science research led to large-scale federal support of academic scientists and to the widespread employment of research scholars in nonacademic settings, as well as to the increasing activity of university professors as consultants and advisers to industrial and governmental institutions.

The Natural Sciences
The first academicians to enjoy federal largess in relation to their research in the post-World War II period were, of course, the natural scientists, whose work had "paid off" so conspicuously in the course of the war effort. During the 1940s and

1950s, it was the natural sciences that received a lion's share of the federal expenditures on university research. And it was scientists in government, and university scientists acting as advisers to government, who effectively shaped federal science policy and exercised control over the allocation of funds to their colleagues. Particularly with the appointment in 1957 of the Special Assistant to the President for Science and Technology and of the President's Science Advisory Committee, scientists—as advocates for science research—enjoyed representation at the highest levels of governmental policy making. As a result of their impressive influence as individuals on government programs, natural scientists had little need for their learned societies to function as advocates for their research interests to federal agencies and Congress. The case was quite different, however, for the social sciences.

The Social Sciences Although the government had drawn upon social science knowledge during World War II to further the war effort and large numbers of clinical psychologists, for example, had continued to work in government agencies (such as the Veterans Administration and the Public Health Service) following the war, it was not until the late 1950s that federal agencies began to show a serious interest in supporting academic social science research. A strong stimulus in this direction was a growing governmental concern for the nation's intransigent social problems, many of which seemed related to rapid technological change in the postwar era. On the assumption that university social scientists could assist with the solution of these problems, the government made available increasing support for social research during the late 1950s and early 1960s. But with this rise of support, the relationship between social scientists, government funding agencies, and Congress became considerably more ambivalent than that established earlier between natural scientists and their federal sponsors.

First of all, social scientists confronted skepticism within government regarding both the validity and the usefulness of the products of their research, which were of less obvious utility, from the layman's perspective, than the technical apparatus so often developed in the natural sciences. Second, those problems to which social scientists addressed themselves were far more controversial, in the early 1960s, than the technical problems being confronted by most natural scientists, kindling fears among government officials of negative congressional repercussions from agency-sponsored social research. One result was the tendency on the part of funding agencies to restrict support to research in politically "safe" areas. Third, the use of human subjects in social research (as well as in some areas of natural science, such as biomedical research) produced anxiety in many legislators and agency officials regarding the ethics of federally sponsored research in these areas. Questions regarding the ethics of research on human behavior were raised, for example, in congressional subcommittee hearings on the invasion of personal privacy by social scientists and led in some instances to restrictions on the use of research instruments and procedures in federally funded social science projects.

While not unconcerned with the ethical problems raised by the government, social scientists themselves were more alarmed by the threat that federal restrictions posed to their research autonomy—autonomy that they considered essential to the advancement of knowledge in their disciplines. The fact that they did not enjoy advisory positions within government (*as advocates for social science research*) of the same status and prestige as those held by "hard" scientists made them particularly vulnerable to the imposition of lay standards on the selection of acceptable areas of research and research methods in government-supported projects. For these reasons, social researchers turned to their learned societies to act as advocates of their professional interests to the federal government. By the mid-1960s, four of the five major social science learned societies in the United States—the American Anthropological Association (AAA), the American Sociological Association (ASA), the American Political Science Association (APSA), and the American Psychological Association (APA)—had established their headquarters in Washington, D.C. [only the American Economic Association (AEA) had not] and had delegated to their office staffs, and to newly created committees on federal relations, the responsibility for monitoring federal activities of potential interest and concern to association members, for urging more equitable support of relatively "deprived" research areas or disciplines, for defending the research autonomy of social scientists against restrictive clauses accompanying federal grants, and for promoting the use of their members as consultants and advisers to governmental agencies.

One major limitation on this type of activity for learned societies, however, has been the fact that monitoring and lobbying government are expensive and time-consuming activities for which three of the four social science associations in Washington (the ASA, APSA, and AAA) have had generally inadequate resources. Only the APA has had the necessary staff and financial means to carry on a continuous and extensive program of federal relations. (For a further discussion, see Bloland, 1968.)

But for the APA, as for the other learned societies in Washington, an additional restraint on lobbying activities or attempts to influence federal legislation has been their special tax status as "educational" and "scientific" organizations.[2] They do not pay federal taxes on their income, and contributions to them are tax deductible, as long as they do not

(i)...devote more than an insubstantial part of their activities to attempting to influence legislation by propaganda or otherwise; or (ii) directly or indirectly...participate in, or intervene in (including the publishing or distributing of statements), any political campaign on behalf of or in opposition to any candidate for public office (Income Tax Regulations, 1967, pp. 33, 435–436).[3]

Thus, learned societies are inhibited both by their special tax status and by a desire to avoid the public image of lobbyists from engaging in overt or conspicuous pressure group activities in their relations with government. Although they have attempted to provide federal agencies and Congress with information regarding legislation that touches their professional concerns, they prefer to testify only by invitation before congressional committees and to emphasize their expertise concerning the needs of social science research, rather than special "interests," as the basis for their role as advocates.

Despite these constraints, the threat of undue governmental influence on the conduct of social research played an important part in making federal relations a central concern of social sci-

[2] See subsections 501(c)3 and 170(c)2 of the Internal Revenue Code.

[3] Professional associations, on the other hand, are covered by subsection 501(c)6 of the Internal Revenue Code, according to which they do not pay federal tax on their income, but contributions made to them are not tax deductible. Under this section of the tax code, no limitations are placed on the political activity of professional societies. Organizations such as the American Medical Association, for example, have openly supported candidates for public office whom they considered to be friendly to their views and have campaigned against candidates whom they regarded as hostile to organized medicine.

ence associations by the mid-1960s and had raised new questions, as well, regarding the appropriate role of learned societies as potential regulatory bodies in relation to the professional activities of their members. Internal debates had begun to take place within social science associations (such as the ASA, the APSA, and the AAA) concerning the need for formal codes of ethical conduct to guide social scientists funded by nonacademic agencies and organizations.

One major issue underlying the new concern with codes of ethics was a conflict between the basic commitment of the social scientist (as it was perceived by many members of the social science disciplines in the mid-1960s) to the "objective" and "value-free" pursuit of knowledge on the one hand, and to the increasing employment of social researchers by mission-oriented government agencies on the other. This conflict was felt more keenly in the social sciences than it was in the natural sciences, despite the greater indebtedness of natural scientists to government for the support of their work. Whereas many social scientists feared the influence of government sponsorship on the very findings of social science research, natural scientists were less prone to such fears—in part because of a greater faith in the methodological precision of their research, and in part because of the less direct relationship that was presumed to exist between their findings and the ideological commitments of the agencies funding their work. In addition, the direct relationship between the work of social scientists and critical social problems made it considerably more difficult for social researchers, than for natural scientists, to disclaim responsibility for the uses to which their research was put or to claim value neutrality in the research process.

Even the conflict between the scientific principle of full disclosure of research findings and the occasional attempts of government to restrict the release of research results to protect agency missions posed a more serious threat to social scientists than it did to natural scientists. Although both groups were deeply concerned with government constraints upon the dissemination of new knowledge, social scientists feared, in addition, that the results of social research lent themselves to potential distortion and misrepresentation by government sponsors, which jeopardized the credibility of the social scientist as well as his contribution to the advancement of his discipline.

Finally, the continued employment of social scientists in intelligence activities for such agencies as the State Department and the Central Intelligence Agency in the postwar period jeopardized the scientific credibility of all American social researchers seeking to gather data in foreign countries and of many engaged in research in the United States as well.

For these reasons, then, social scientists, more than natural scientists, saw in federal sponsorship a serious threat to their integrity as research scholars and to the development of their disciplines. One response to this threat was to turn to their learned societies to take the lead in defining the responsibilities of the social science researcher in his relationship to his discipline, his colleagues, and agencies financing his work.

Spurred by the public scandal surrounding Project Camelot in 1965 and by subsequent exposure of CIA sponsorship of programs at Michigan State University and MIT (among other incidents), ethics committees within the APSA, the ASA, and the AAA gave special attention to the need for guidelines for social researchers supported by nonacademic organizations.[4] All stressed the primacy of the principle of full disclosure, according to which social scientists should be willing to reveal all sources of support for their research, its full nature and purposes, and all conditions placed upon the conduct of their work by a supporting agency. It was uniformly suggested that social scientists should refuse support from organizations that place unacceptable restrictions on the conduct of research or on the full release of results or that desire to conceal their sponsorship. Further, any complicity of social scientists with intelligence activities or with other attempts to obtain information for nonprofessional purposes was strongly condemned.

Response within these three learned societies to the proposed adoption of formal codes of ethics, to be enforced by formal sanctions, was by no means unanimous, although the AAA had gone farther than the other two societies by the late 1960s in gaining membership approval of a formal statement of ethical principles. In neither the APSA nor the ASA had such agreement been reached by the latter part of the decade, but in both

---

[4] Faced much earlier with the need for standards of ethical practice for its clinical and counseling psychologist members, the APA had established an extensive code of ethics, and machinery to enforce this code, in 1953.

organizations ethics committees continued to labor at the task of defining standards of conduct for the social researcher, considering and giving formal opinions on specific questions of ethical conduct brought before them by association members (see Orans, 1973, pp. 51–80).

The Humanities Meanwhile, the situation in the humanities with regard to federal support and federal relations activity was different from that in either the natural or the social sciences. During the period of government largess to scientific research programs, research in the humanities enjoyed only meager federal support—consisting in large part of such annual awards to individual scholars as Fulbright and Woodrow Wilson fellowships. As a result, learned societies representing the humanities were called upon intermittently to express member dissatisfaction with the level of federal aid to their disciplines, but there was little basis for most of these associations to establish permanent machinery to promote their research interests to government.[5]

The most concerted association efforts on behalf of government support for the humanities were launched by the American Council of Learned Societies (ACLS), through its 1964 Commission on the Humanities (sponsored in conjunction with the Council of Graduate Schools in the United States and the United Chapters of Phi Beta Kappa), which was a strong force in the creation of the National Endowment for the Humanities in 1965. The continued leadership of the ACLS as an advocate to the government of the value of humanistic scholarship seems to have mitigated the necessity for its member societies to establish independent machinery for that purpose.

[5] Among the humanities, history has maintained the closest and most continual ties with federal agencies, primarily because of the ongoing need of historians for access to government documents and particularly to the Library of Congress and the National Archives, as resources for historical research. Thus, the American Historical Association has its headquarters in Washington and has regularly acted through its Committee on the Historian and the Federal Government to press government to make available to historians the federal records and materials which their research requires. In 1970, it requested that its joint committee with the Organization of American Historians (the Joint AHA-OAH Coordinating Committee of Historians on Federal Government Relations) devise machinery for investigating "complaints against public or private repositories, involving the discriminatory treatment of researchers or the unwarranted denial of access to documents" (Ward, 1970, p. 6).

In the period between World War II and the mid-1960s, learned societies acquired greater monetary resources as a result of increased income from membership dues and of grants and contracts from foundations and government. Most societies developed more elaborate office facilities, required for the maintenance of increasingly complex administrative structures. Many learned societies assumed a central role in allocating national prestige within the disciplines, and a number of these organizations also assumed important representative functions for their members—in relation to the government, foundations, and industry—expanding their range of concerns to include the relationship of the disciplinary professions to publics outside the university, in contrast to their more exclusively intellectual focus earlier in the century.

These various forms of growth and expansion created a burgeoning demand for association leadership during the 1950s and 1960s and steadily enhanced the power and influence of the oligarchies that continued to manage organizational affairs.

A proliferation of committees, which involved larger numbers of members—in an advisory capacity—in the policy process, was one outgrowth of the need for more concerted attention to policy issues. Another was the allocation of an increasing amount of council business to an executive committee (which could meet more frequently than a full board of directors or council and could provide more regular support and guidance to the executive secretary), which further centralized formal decision-making processes within associations.

In many cases, the association presidency became a more influential post, requiring a greater expenditure of time and effort and considerable organizational skill. In selecting among the most eminent scholars in their respective fields, nominating committees inevitably began to consider organizational ability and commitment to be relevant criteria in the choice of association officers. Thus, candidates came to be drawn more and more often from the members of key committees or the council, where they had gained familiarity with and demonstrated some skill at handling association affairs. It also became common practice to enhance the effectiveness of the president by involving him for a year or two in the governance of the organization as its vice-president or president-elect before placing upon his shoulders the full responsibilities of the association's highest office.

Despite the fact that association memberships grew and diversified and that more and more influence over external and internal professional affairs accrued to a small body of association leaders, little fundamental change occurred in the criteria or procedures according to which these officials were selected or in the way in which major policy decisions were made within disciplinary associations. Governance procedures continued to reflect the assumption—deeply rooted in the value system in the disciplines—that association memberships were essentially homogeneous in their commitment to the advancement of knowledge and that questions concerning the nature and development of the disciplinary professions could most appropriately be answered by those elite members of each of the academic fields whose judgments were held to constitute scholarly authority. The very concentration of power in the hands of so few association officers seemed merely to mirror the tendency in the disciplines, themselves, for rewards and recognition to accrue to relatively few scholars (Zuckerman, 1970).

Efforts were made to widen participation in annual meetings and to provide more diverse avenues for publishing scholarly work. Nominating committees began to show a deliberate concern for achieving greater "balance" in the selection of candidates for association office and to ensure representation of different geographical regions of the country, of different disciplinary specialties, and of different types of higher educational institutions. Nevertheless, scholars from a relatively small number of high-prestige, research-oriented universities seemed to many members of the disciplines to play a disproportionately large role in governing their learned societies and to monopolize association journals and annual meetings. There developed a widespread sense on the part of association members in many of the disciplines that their learned societies were increasingly controlled by self-perpetuating elites or had fallen into the hands of an "establishment" that was geographically based on the East Coast (sometimes including parts of the Midwest and California), where the greatest number of prestigious universities are located.

The existence of such suspicions among association members was openly acknowledged, for example, in the report of the outgoing president of the American Sociological Association in 1964, who referred to "certain views disturbing to the President that have been current among the members, ranging from the view that the Association is dominated by an 'Eastern clique' among its officers to the probably more realistic view that the officers have been somewhat out of touch with the regional societies" (Homans, 1964, p. 895). And Somit and Tanenhaus wrote in 1967 of the "steady, if muted, drumfire of criticism that the [American Political Science] Association has become progressively less democratic, and that control of the profession has fallen into the hands of an Establishment, however defined" (pp. 154–155). In the latter case, a major point of dissatisfaction (as indicated by a 1963 survey of APSA members) was the view that a small clique controlled the assignment of participants to key panels at association meetings. Another common complaint from members of many disciplines was that their specialties were denied adequate representation in association publications; and tension within a discipline regarding theoretical and methodological cleavages has at times been greatly exacerbated by the accusation of bias on the part of association editorial boards.

While such tensions did occasionally erupt into open disputes and challenge the apparent monopoly of elite groups within the disciplines over organizational resources, they did not lead to a concerted attack on the legitimacy of the reward structure or on the role of associations in shaping and reinforcing dominant patterns of reward distribution. Nor did they inspire organized member protest against association governance procedures. Well into the 1960s, business meetings continued to be sparsely attended; nominees for office were very rarely challenged by member-sponsored candidates; and voter participation in mail-ballot elections was still extremely limited. Nevertheless, this latent discontent was to be an important source of momentum at the end of the decade for change in traditional patterns of association governance.

CONCLUSION Despite the relatively uncontested processes through which disciplinary associations expanded their facilities, their activities, and their functions in the postwar period, the growth and enhanced influence of learned societies had created two organizational disjunctures that were to make these associations particularly vulnerable to the radical critique of the late 1960s.

First, oligarchic control over the distribution of association resources had begun to be a source of discontent among association memberships as these memberships diversified—both in terms of the range of higher education institutions and other organizations by which they were employed and in terms of their increasingly specialized research interests—and as association leaders began to wield increasing influence on the structure of career opportunities and on the directions of growth and change in these professions.

Second, many of these associations had become enmeshed with government agencies, foundations, and other types of organizations in the postwar years, recognizing no inconsistency between these ties and their commitment as disciplinary associations to detachment from social and political affairs. These relationships were defined exclusively in terms of the positive conditions they were thought to create for the advancement of knowledge in the disciplines (and for the growth of public recognition of the value and importance of the products of research), on the assumption that new knowledge could only contribute to the public good. Little attention was devoted, during this period, to the social and political implications of association ties with particular mission-oriented organizations (such as the Department of Defense) as a result of this assumption and the widespread view that scholars and their organizations could remain "value-neutral" regardless of their sources of support or of the institutional context within which they carried on their work.

The radical attack of the 1960s on the legitimacy of the government and other dominant institutions in the society and upon the very concept of value neutrality or political detachment for the natural scientist, social scientist, or scholar in the humanities was to hold up for more critical scrutiny the relationships that had developed between learned societies—and the disciplines they represent—and the dominant institutional and ideological interests in society. Social science associations were particularly vulnerable to the radical argument that these ties had influenced the very content of the work that these organizations promoted in their respective fields, and it was within this group of disciplines that the radical critique found its first expression in American learned societies. The radical movement also had a strong and significant counterpart in the humanities, although its impact on natural science associations was less extensive.

3. The Caucus Movement

The first concerted challenge to the traditional ethos and governance structure of American learned societies was issued in 1967 and 1968 by groups of academics and intellectuals who felt compelled by events of the decade to establish a more direct relationship between their scholarly work, their participation in professional organizations, and their deep concern for the major social and political issues confronting American society. The new level of political commitment among many learned-society members, which was to find expression in the creation of "radical" caucuses within disciplinary associations, had its roots in several diverse movements of the 1960s: the civil rights movement in the South, the peace movement in the North, the student movement on university campuses, and the more general thrust toward cultural liberation among American youth.

By the latter part of the 1960s, however, the focal issue around which the broadest protest movement had taken form, both within the academic community and among the general public, was the Vietnam War. The steady escalation of United States military involvement in Southeast Asia, particularly since 1965, had engendered public dismay and outrage and prompted two massive demonstrations in New York City and San Francisco in the spring of 1967 and an even more massive march on Washington in October of that year. By 1968, numerous racial uprisings in American cities had become linked with the war in new left ideology as closely related symptoms of a fundamentally imperialist and racist society. Together these issues provided the cornerstone for a broadening radical critique of the corporate and military structure in America.

Frustrated by the lack of effective channels through which to exert organized political force within the existing political system, many academic scholars—and particularly large numbers of graduate students and young faculty members—felt it imperative that the pressing social-political crisis be recognized within the organizational and institutional structures of their disciplines as a focus for the concentration of both intellectual and monetary resources. They decried the failure of their learned societies and their disciplines generally to devote serious study and discussion to the major problems confronting American society; and they challenged the overspecialization of the academic disciplines, their deceptive claim to value neutrality, and their use of specialized knowledge to support the dominant institutional and ideological interests of the society rather than to promote and direct social change.

Central to this challenge was a critique of the traditional reward structure within the disciplines, which placed heavy constraints on social criticism through its exclusive recognition of scholarship alleged to be value-neutral and politically detached. Perceived as formal embodiments of this academic reward system and as key agencies in the distribution of resources within the disciplines, learned societies came to be viewed as relevant arenas for action by dissident scholars and scientists who argued that reform of these organizations—democratization of their governance structures, severance of their ties with the government and other "establishment" institutions, and reform of their traditional patterns of resource allocation—was an important prerequisite to any significant change in the disciplines themselves. These associations were also viewed as a logical avenue of attack on a professional opportunity structure that had consistently discriminated against blacks and members of other minority groups as well as against women. Thus, it was to the reform of these organizations that many radical, women's, and minority-group caucuses first bent their efforts.

PARTICIPANTS IN THE CAUCUS MOVEMENT
Not all the participants in the "radical" caucus movement of the late 1960s and early 1970s can be characterized as *radical* in the sense that they were ultimately committed to profound political, social, or intellectual transformations. Basic distinctions will be made here between (1) caucus members whose social and intellectual goals were radical, or revolutionary; (2) those whose objectives could be more accurately described as "liberal

reform" of society, of their disciplines, and of their disciplinary associations; and (3) women and members of racial, ethnic, and other relatively excluded groups within the disciplines whose purposes related explicitly to the enhancement of career opportunities in their fields. A further distinction between two different types of radicals is useful here. These will be designated *radical activists* and *radical intellectuals.*

Within the social sciences and humanities, a major objective of radicals who participated in the caucus movement was to change the theoretical and methodological focus of their disciplines. Although radical activists and radical intellectuals shared this objective, they can be distinguished from each other generally on the basis of fundamental differences in (1) their conception of the nature of science or of theory building and (2) the nature of their commitment to academic organizations as a setting for the pursuit of intellectual careers.

Radical Activists The most visible and vociferous dissidents in the early stages of caucus activity within learned societies were a group of graduate students and young professors identifying themselves with the New Left, whose critique of the disciplines and of the "academy" centered on the fundamental supposition within these established structures that political activism has no part in the professional role of the academic social scientist or scholar. Arguing the obligation of the intellectual to be politically involved and to take responsibility for translating theory into practice, these activists conceived of theory development in the social sciences and humanities as being inextricably bound up with social action, accepting the Marxist premise that the basis of social analysis is praxis.

Having rejected the concept of science or academic scholarship as activities having unique or distinctive features that require their insulation from political life, the radical activists had relatively little commitment or loyalty to the institutionalized norms and values of the disciplines or to the organizations that have provided an insular setting for the conduct of academic research—to universities, to learned societies, or to the disciplines as career systems. At one extreme, some members of this group argued for the destruction of these organizations and institutions. The more moderate and prevalent position held, however, that the work of the radical scholar-activist could advantageously be carried on within these structures, even though the activist is committed first to social transformation (to "the revolution") and only second to the pursuit of an academic career that would demand his submitting to the standards of his professional colleagues. One politically active sociologist has asserted, for example:

No Marxist ought to publish for the sake of publishing; no Marxist ought to pursue his studies as a "career." . . .The demands of the immediate struggle become the primary focus of the activists' analysis and publication. . . . Since one does not struggle in order to publish, but publishes in order to struggle, the activist role is in contradiction to the "publish or perish" expectations of mainstream sociology (Dixon, 1972, p. 14).

Such an orientation toward the requirements of an academic career has tended to place the radical activist in a highly precarious position in his university department, to isolate him from his colleagues, and often to result in efforts to remove him formally from his academic post. Nevertheless, the same writer continues:

Activists recognize the need for contemplation, for periodic withdrawal from immediate social action in order to further theoretical mastery and to systematize and integrate practical knowledge with the existing body of theory. Such "stolen moments" are very precious, and a university position is one of the chief means by which activists are able to accomplish much study and writing. It is one of the chief reasons why Marxist activists seek to remain within universities (ibid., p. 14).

In addition, many activists have considered the role of radical teacher to be a vitally important medium through which to work toward long-range social objectives, a critical reason for continuing to work within academic institutions.

The relationship between the radical activist and his university was an issue of key importance to members of the New University Conference (NUC), which served as the national focal organization for many activist university teachers between 1968 and 1972, and which proclaimed itself a "national organization of radicals who work in, around, and in spite of institutions of higher education" and characterized its members as "political activists who define their work in education as part of the broader struggle for radical social change in the United States" (New University Conference, n.d., p. 2).

One founding member of the NUC, Staughton Lynd, argued strongly that academic culture and the constraints of an academic career were virtually prohibitive of effective radical action, and that the radical activist could, at best, use the university only temporarily as a base of activity and a source of income (Birnbaum, 1970, p. 62).

While this argument received strong support during the first years of NUC growth and activity, it was soon to become irrelevant to the material conditions facing radicals in the 1970s. With the eventual disappearance of all potential for a broad revolutionary movement with which radical scholar-activists could ally themselves and with the submergence of radical organizations outside of the university, it became increasingly necessary for radical activists to accept—and try to maintain—their university posts as a permanent source of financial support. Under these circumstances, most activists turned to radical teaching and to efforts to unionize academic faculties as the only available means for furthering their social objectives. The job pressure on such activists was severe, however, and employment pressure on organizers of campus chapters is widely held to have been responsible for the demise of the NUC in 1972.

Between 1968 and 1972, however, the NUC provided an important organizational base for the initiation and coordination of radical caucus activities—particularly within learned societies representing the humanities (such as the Modern Language Association and the American Historical Association) and also within the American Association for the Advancement of Science—with the NUC national meetings serving as occasions for the formulation of radical caucus strategies and programs. It was a general assumption of NUC members and other radical activist caucus members that, far from being politically neutral or "detached" organizations, their learned societies were implicitly engaged in supporting the dominant institutional and ideological interests in the United States and that it should be their function, on the contrary, to generate social change. Thus, radical activists called upon disciplinary associations to make public policy statements on critical social issues such as the Vietnam War and to divert their resources to the support of action or action-research programs geared toward transforming the society.

Radical Intellectuals Generally distinguishable from the first category of political activists was a significant number of caucus members who defined themselves first as *intellectuals* rather than as activists (although many of them had undoubtedly been politically active in the course of their academic careers) and whose primary identification tended to be with their disciplines—as bodies of knowledge, as systems of social values and norms, and as career systems—rather than with groups or organizations comprising the New Left. This group shared with radical activist caucus members their deep concern for the social and political crisis confronting the society and urged that academic scholars be far more directly concerned in their work with contemporary social problems and issues and that they take greater responsibility for the uses to which their research products were put. But, in contrast to radical activists, members of this group defined differently the very nature of the theory-building process, placing greater faith in the insight to be derived from research and analysis conducted in the insular setting of the university and within the institutional context of an academic career. Less inclined to integrate theory and action within their own professional lives, these radical intellectuals characteristically argued:

The prime objective of struggle within disciplines and within the professions which give the disciplines organizational form is the advancement of theory. The first obligation to a radical movement owed by radical intellectuals is criticism and counsel founded on adequate theory.... [Caucus] activities within these associations and professions must first and foremost serve the theoretical goal of making the disciplines places where we can do our work, including of course work between teachers and students (Kettler, 1970b, p. 44).

The mission of the radical intellectual, then, was the development of a critique of the theoretical and methodological perspectives currently predominating in the disciplines (perspectives that were uniformly compatible with the prevailing stress on value neutrality and upon social detachment in the academic fields), and the creation of new paradigms and modes of analysis able to provide greater insight into contemporary social events and to offer, as well, a theoretical foundation for programs of social action. Radical intellectuals believed this process of theory development to be a uniquely rational and introspective activity proceeding most appropriately in settings that provide insulation from the passions of political life. But they additionally argued the necessity for reforming academic structures that offer such a potential setting, seeking to make them more egalitarian and to create in them conditions more conducive to the involvement of the scholar in social criticism and in the development of radical theory.

In comparison to radical activists, members of the caucus movement who can be characterized as radical intellectuals tended to be somewhat older and more firmly established in careers in their respective fields and exhibited a greater inclination to maintain amicable collegial relationships with members of the "establishment" in their universities and learned societies. Fewer of the members of this group were disposed to engage in militant confrontations with association leadership.

For both radical activists and radical intellectuals, the importance of learned societies lay in their presumed influence on the kinds of work granted recognition within the disciplines. Reform of these organizations was seen as an avenue through which to alter the dominant patterns of reward distribution and to secure greater professional recognition and financial support for socially "relevant" research. However, while radical activists were inclined to use their associations as vehicles for the public expression of ideas and of social outrage, radical intellectuals in the caucus movement were generally more intent upon achieving internal intellectual reform, and sought to gain acceptance of contemporary social problems and issues as a legitimate focus for work presented at annual association meetings and published in major association journals and to commit association and disciplinary resources to intensive examination of the nature and origins of the crisis facing the United States.

Radical activists and intellectuals alike argued the necessity for wider participation in the decision-making processes within their association and further urged that association governance procedures be "politicized," in the sense that the political position of candidates for association office be granted overt and central importance as a basis for their election or selection and that the annual business meeting be used as a forum for the open debate of contemporary social-political questions (which would make it a vehicle for consciousness raising among association members).

The distinction between radical activists and radical intellectuals is most useful in relation to the study of dissidence in the social sciences and the humanities. In the natural sciences, the dominant theoretical paradigms have not been the focus of a radical criticism emanating from *within* the disciplines, and so there is no exact equivalent within the scientific fields to either the radical activist, who seeks the integration of theory and practice, or the radical intellectual, whose primary commitment is to the revision of the theoretical structures within which he carries on his scholarly or scientific work. Rather, the focus of the radical attack within the natural sciences was upon the failure of moral responsibility within the scientific community regarding the selection of research problems to be pursued and the uses to which scientific knowledge is put.

Nevertheless, a distinction holds in these fields between those dissident scientists who have retained a primary identification with their disciplines and pursued traditional academic or professional careers (which necessarily involves a rigorous commitment to the advancement of theory) and radical scientists who have tended to eschew academic institutions and the pursuit of professional careers within them and who are more directly dedicated to the *application* of scientific knowledge for the relief of social problems (working, for example, through such organizations as Scientists and Engineers for Social and Political Action, also known as Science for the People).

In sciences such as physics, it is striking that far fewer radicals have managed to combine strong political commitments with academic careers than is true in the social sciences and humanities, most importantly, it would seem, because of the lack of direct relationship between political activity and analysis on the one hand and the development of the major disciplinary paradigms on the other. Thus, within the natural sciences, the concerns of radicals have been even more readily defined as irrelevant and inappropriate to the pursuit of professional careers than has been the case in other academic disciplines. Consequently, far fewer radicals have attempted to work *within* scientific learned societies (which have, as a rule, been less hospitable to radical activity than have those representing the humanities and the social sciences). There have, nevertheless, been significant attempts by radicals in the hard sciences to introduce political issues into the content of association journals and of papers and panel discussions at association meetings to commit their associations to public stands on controversial social-political issues, and to politicize the governance processes in these organizations.

Left-Liberal Reformers More similar in style and orientation to radical intellectuals than to radical activists, left-liberal caucus members also tended to be well established in intellectual and scientific careers and strongly committed to the disciplines and to the institutions and organizations that house them. They, too, have argued the need to urge these organizations and institutions toward more direct involvement in, and responsibility for, social-political events and issues. But despite their vociferous protest against the Vietnam War and their concern for civil rights and for matters relating to academic freedom, what has distinguished these caucus members most importantly from their radical colleagues has been a narrower vision of the social, intellectual, and organizational transformation to be achieved by caucus activity. Committed neither to social revolution nor to radical revision of the theoretical structures within their disciplines, they were primarily dedicated to encouraging the formal study of public policy problems within their fields and to creating association committees to investigate such issues as discrimination in the disciplines, graduate student problems, questions relating to academic freedom, and the like.

Like their more radical colleagues, left-liberal caucus members also argued the necessity for democratizing association governance procedures and increasing member participation on all levels of association activity; but they differed from radical scholars and scientists on the issue of politicizing learned societies in a broader sense. They were more likely to defend traditional scholarly criteria (against more overtly political criteria) as a basis for the selection of association officers and to urge more circumscribed and formal procedures (such as the creation of special panels at association meetings or of special committees) for the introduction of political questions into association affairs.

Women, Blacks, Ethnic Groups, and Members of the Academic Proletariat

Finally, a large number of dissidents who lent support to the caucus movement in the late 1960s were most directly concerned with alleviating inequities in the opportunity structure in their disciplines and associations. Protesting their underrepresentation in association leadership positions and in association activities, women, members of racial and ethnic minority groups, and academicians from relatively low-prestige institutions—particularly scholars and scientists from institutions in the South and Midwest—saw reform of association governance structures and procedures as a means of enhancing their career opportunities in the disciplines.

Where separate groups formed explicitly to challenge the opportunity structure in their disciplines, however, as did caucuses of women, blacks, and Chicanos, for example, internal tensions often emerged as a result of the simultaneous commitment of many of their members to radical social goals—a commitment that was sometimes difficult to reconcile with efforts to enhance access to careers and to positions of influence within existing professional structures. (Tensions were also manifest in the relations between black caucuses and explicitly radical groups, which expressed support of black caucus objectives but confessed little cooperative interaction with them.)

Women and racial and ethnic groups joined the radical assault on elitism in the governance of disciplinary associations, demanding wider participation in association decision-making processes. And these dissidents also called upon their learned societies, most specifically, to adopt policies discouraging and condemning discrimination in the disciplines and to devote resources to encouraging members of underrepresented groups to enter the disciplines and to provide them with compensatory advantages in their pursuit of scholarly or scientific careers.

EARLY COALITIONS

Thus, dissident scholars and scientists with diverse perspectives and ideological commitments formed broad coalitions in the early history of the caucus movement, making it difficult for both association and caucus leadership to discern which proportion of their memberships could be counted on to support programs for fundamental organizational, intellectual, or social change. The varied composition of such coalitions was to gradually reveal itself and to diminish over several years' time as an outcome of continuous internal debate over questions of caucus strategy and goals.

Perhaps the most decisive issue over which conflict was to persist within many radical caucuses was the question of the effectiveness and importance—symbolic or instrumental—of learned societies as vehicles for promoting social or intellectual change and of the ultimate value of investing time and energy in prolonged and involved programs to reform these organizations. The strongest argument for the significance of disciplinary associations as arenas for sustained caucus activity was the presumed influence of these organizations in intradisciplinary affairs. What was far more ambiguous was their potential influence in a wider social-political sphere. Thus, while participants in the caucus movement tended to agree on the importance of wider participation in learned-society governance and activities, there were vast differences among these dissidents in the extent to which they were willing to focus their own limited resources on a prolonged and intensive effort to gain influence or to promote change in these organizations.

These differences were somewhat obscured in 1967 and 1968, however, by the relatively easy success of many caucuses in their first attempts to affect association policy. A combination of factors gave the early impression that caucus activity might produce dramatic results in this context with a relatively minor investment of time and energy. First was the obvious vulnerability of organizations whose important policy decisions were made at open—and very poorly attended—business meetings. All that seemed required of caucus groups seeking an impact on association affairs was adequate attendance by their members and supporters at the annual business meeting. And second, widespread sentiment against the Vietnam War, combined with general dissatisfaction among discipline members with the elitism of their professional societies, gave the impression of strong potential support for a wide range of caucus programs. It was not until the power of the business meeting had been diluted or eliminated (as it was almost universally) in response to radical activity there and the limits of association membership support for caucus reform had been clearly revealed, that important distinctions began to emerge between caucus members who saw disciplinary associations as critical arenas for *sustained* efforts to achieve change and those who quickly came to see other groups and settings as more relevant and strategic for the achievement of their long-range objectives.

DECLINE OF CAUCUS ACTIVISM Insofar as any consistent pattern emerged in the attitudes of different types of caucus members toward the centrality of learned societies as loci for dissident activity, it was generally true that radical activists showed the briefest interest in transforming these organizations. Concerned from the beginning that organizing within the associations would leave radicals particularly vulnerable to cooptation by disciplinary "establishments"—that caucuses operating exclusively in this context would inevitably begin to imitate the elitist and bureaucratic style of the organizations they sought to change—activists intensified their arguments against a continued focus on learned societies as bases for activism as the limitations on their use for social or political ends became clear. At this point, activists began to argue that the stakes no longer justified the effort and urged a redefinition of caucus purposes and reorganization of these groups outside the framework of establishment organizations. Independence from these "mother structures," it was argued, would divert caucus energies from fruitless efforts to effect organizational reform and would facilitate alliances with other radical caucuses in the disciplines as well as with more activist groups comprising the New Left.

Where the activist perspective did *not* predominate (as in the case of the Caucus for a New Political Science), activist members began to drop out of the caucus movement altogether. Where their perspective *was* predominant, however, (as in the case of the Radical Caucus in English and the Modern Languages) radical caucuses began to assume an independent structure—with a strong regional locus, due to the lack of available travel funds for nationally dispersed members—and met frequently during the periods between national learned-society conventions. Nevertheless, even as their attention turned from efforts to transform disciplinary associations, they continued to use annual association meetings as important occasions for national gatherings of like-minded radicals and for recruitment of new members.

As a result of the declining interest of activists in disciplinary associations after 1970, the tone and style of caucus activity changed noticeably, with a reduction in the tendency toward militant confrontations with association leadership.

The greater number of radical intellectuals and left-liberal reformers, on the other hand, who tended to identify more strongly with careers in the disciplines, continued to view learned societies as vitally important for the achievement of intellectual and professional reform and argued the necessity for prolonged efforts to gain influence or power in these organizations. Thus, these caucus members were more likely to continue into the 1970s to organize alternative panels at association meetings, to work for the election of radicals and reformers to association leadership positions, and the like.

Many of those caucus members concerned centrally with equalization of career opportunities also demonstrated a persistent willingness to work within learned societies, a tendency that is partly explained by the fact that their demands were among the first to be granted legitimacy by association membership and leadership alike. Thus, women's caucuses in particular have continued into the present decade to be one of the most vital remnants of the caucus movement, with steadily growing memberships, continuous expansion of activities, and notable successes in their impact on association policies and programs.

THREE CASE STUDIES   The interplay of various subgroups in shaping the character and program of radical caucuses and the impact of these bodies on the structure and ethos of learned societies provide the focus for the three case studies in this volume. The data for these case studies were obtained from the numerous periodicals, newsletters, and annual reports published by each of the three associations and from various publications of dissident groups within these organizations. Interviews were also conducted between 1970 and 1973 with learned-society officers and committee members as well as representatives of the various caucuses that emerged in these associations in the late 1960s. (See Appendix A for a list of interviewees.)

4. Dissent in the American Political Science Association

The American Political Science Association (APSA) came into existence in 1903, an offshoot of the American Economic Association and the American Historical Association, "to encourage the study of Political Science." The offices of the association and the editorial board of its official journal, the *American Political Science Review* (*APSR*), have been dominated by academic political scientists throughout its history. The academics also constituted a majority of the association's membership by 1920 and 70 percent of its membership by the early 1960s (Somit & Tanenhaus, 1967, pp. 55 and 146).

The APSA grew dramatically in the post-World War II period, with an increase in membership from 5,126 to 18,000 between 1950 and 1970 (see Table 1, p. 12). Its assets, based on income from membership dues and a number of foundation grants, increased from $47,783 in 1954 to $2,500,000 by 1969 ("Report of the Treasurer...," 1969, p. 560).

Although the scholarly and systematic advancement of knowledge has always been a primary objective of the APSA and of the political science profession, there has also been a strong sense of responsibility among American political scientists for educating the nation's youth for democratic citizenship, and, in the same vein, a marked inclination for political scientists to take an active personal interest in public affairs. In their characterization of the discipline Somit and Tanenhaus (1967, pp. 45–47) write:

In one respect American political science is unique—it has assumed responsibility for transmitting to the nation's youth the knowledge and the patriotic sentiments deemed essential for the successful functioning of our democratic system. Almost from the beginning, the obligation to prepare college students for their future roles as citizens and leaders was urged upon the profession. . . . From its very inception, then, the profession was committed to the pursuit of truth and to the propagation of democratic values and practices.

For many years, this commitment to education for democratic citizenship found overt expression in the work of major APSA committees as well as in the content of annual meetings and of association journals. At the same time, the interest of political scientists in current political affairs and in questions of public policy was also reflected in a variety of association programs.

It was not until the behavioral revolution in political science of the late 1940s and early 1950s that the scientific study of politics won clear hegemony over these extrascientific pursuits as the major thrust for the further development of the field and as the central preoccupation of its learned society. Proponents of the behavioral orientation—and its claim to value neutrality and detachment in the study of politics—gradually came to monopolize leadership positions in the association. Their work filled the pages of the *APSR*, and their "scientific" concerns set the tone for the majority of papers and panels at the annual meetings.

RELATIONS WITH THE FEDERAL GOVERNMENT
During the same period, the association came to act in an increasingly wide range of capacities as liaison between the political science profession and government institutions. This role was implicitly justified by the "neutrality" and "detachment" of the association as a scholarly and scientific organization. The APSA sponsored, for example, a Congressional Fellowship Program, funded by the Ford Foundation, to bring young scholars and journalists to Washington to take part in the legislative process as interns in the offices of senators and congressmen. It presented Congressional Distinguished Service Awards to "honor legislators for distinguished Congressional services and 'to dramatize the crucial role of a freely elected legislative body in maintaining the values and processes of our democratic society' " ("Report of the Executive Director, " 1969, p. 515). It sponsored a Congressional Staff Fellowship designed to raise the professional competence of congressional staff by placing them in an academic setting to study and conduct research related to

their congressional responsibilities, and it held orientation seminars every two years for freshman congressmen.

Of direct importance for both the financial status and prestige of the discipline was the work of the Washington-based executive secretary of the APSA in winning recognition for political scientists within government agencies. Most notably, this officer played a critical role in establishing political science as a behavioral discipline eligible for inclusion in National Science Foundation programs of research support.

INFLUENCE WITHIN THE FIELD In addition to this liaison function with the government, the association assumed an increasingly influential role within political science in the postwar period, as the success of more and more careers in this academic field (as in others) came to depend upon achieving national recognition. In dispensing fellowships within the profession, in determining the panel participants at association meetings, in selecting the papers for publication in the highly prestigious *APSR*, and in advising political science departments seeking to fill professorial posts, the association played a vital part in the allocation of rewards within the discipline. One critic of this organizational role argued that "there is almost no way of becoming an established political scientist without accepting the tangible rewards that the APSA, and only the APSA, can provide. Without the Association, there is no career; with it, only an absence of intelligence or an excess of integrity stand in the way" (Wolfe, 1969, p. 357). The APSA has also been described as an organization "whose agencies go far towards defining the professional standards by which ambitious departments gauge themselves (and which they use as levers in their dealings with university administrations)" and which can significantly influence departmental policies with respect to "diversity, critical independence, innovation, and related values" (Kettler, 1969*a*).

It is indicative of the influence of the APSA on the development of the field that the rapid success of the behavioral revolution in the early 1950s is widely attributed to the support that the behavioral approach received from the APSA executive director, Evron Kirkpatrick. One recent APSA president asserted:

Where headquarters makes a great difference, and where executive directors,etc., make a great deal of difference, is not just in change but in the *rate* of change, the rate of acceptance of new ideas. Invention of new concepts is unrelated to the central headquarters. But the rate of transformation of the discipline is decisively a part of central headquarters. In this case, the central headquarters was very influential in the change to behavioralism (Interview with David Easton, 1970).

Once committed to a behavioral orientation, however, the APSA demonstrated much less inclination to foster change in the political science profession in succeeding decades and came to appear to dissidents of the late 1960s as a major bulwark of the status quo in the discipline and, indirectly, in American politics. But because its impressive influence on the intellectual climate in political science had been demonstrated, the APSA became the focus of attempts to reform—and in some instances to *transform*—that discipline.

THE CAUCUS FOR A NEW POLITICAL SCIENCE The September 1967 meetings of the APSA followed a year of intensive escalation of the Vietnam War, of massive national demonstrations against United States involvement in Southeast Asia, and of riots in Newark and Detroit.

In addition, members of the APSA had learned in February of that year that the association's executive director and its treasurer and counsel also held positions as president and vice-president, respectively, of a nonprofit research organization that had "received some funds from foundations said to have received funds from Central Intelligence Agency sources" ("Report of the Executive Committee," 1967, p. 565). Two months later, an ad hoc committee of past APSA presidents reported to the association membership that although the research organization in question had, indeed, received grants from foundations reported to be CIA conduits, it saw no evidence that the APSA had been used for intelligence purposes or that any APSA policy regarding the outside activities of its staff had been violated, and it wished to commend the two officers in question for their "great services" to the APSA (ibid., p. 566).

The committee's vote of confidence did not, however, reflect the views of all the APSA members who attended the annual meetings of the association that September. Controversy over this episode was partially responsible for bringing about a dramatic increase in attendance at the business meeting that year, where, caucus members later argued, the matter was further whitewashed by the association leadership.

This affair is widely cited by caucus members as a "precipitating issue" in the formation of the Caucus for a New Political Science (CNPS) in the hours following the Chicago business meeting, although it did far more to raise the level of indignation of dissident APSA members than to focus their protest against APSA leadership. A more direct focus was provided by the summary way in which an amendment on academic freedom (which condemned efforts by the House Un-American Activities Committee to obtain membership lists of campus organizations) was ruled out of order at that 1967 business meeting on the grounds that it was "political" in nature. In support of this ruling it was argued that the association was prohibited by its constitution from adopting positions on any political issues not "immediately concerned with its direct purpose" as a learned society, and that any change in this policy would jeopardize the tax exempt status of the organization and subject it to internal division and factionalism (Bay, 1968, p. 36).

Convinced of an "across the board effort" at the business meeting and the APSA convention generally to "preclude formal study and discussion of all of the great social and political dilemmas facing American democracy today" (Bayer et al., 1968, p. 38), a steadily growing number of dissident political scientists met three times in the next 36 hours, drew up a caucus membership list of over 200 names, elected an executive committee of 13, and adopted several resolutions. The first of these, the caucus's resolution of purposes, indicted the APSA for consistently failing "at its conventions and in its journal . . . to study in a radically critical spirit, either the great crises of the day or the inherent weaknesses of the American political system," and committed the caucus to promoting "a new concern in the Association for our great social crises and a new and broader opportunity for us all to fulfill, as scholars, our obligations to society and to science" (ibid., p. 39).

Discussion at those first three meetings of the caucus, and the subsequent reflection of caucus members on the events of the 1967 APSA convention, contributed to the development of a coherent radical critique of the intellectual content of political science as a discipline, of the role of the association in perpetuating the hegemony of one theoretical-methodological "school" within the discipline, and of the role of both the discipline and the association in supporting the status quo in American politics. While not all the members of the caucus subscribed to all the aspects of this critique, it does represent the basic assumptions underlying the activity of the caucus from 1967 to 1972.

The discipline

Radical political scientists indicted their discipline on several levels for its failure to comprehend or reflect the reality of American politics, to criticize dominant institutions and established social policies, and to offer radical alternatives to a system presently in turmoil. The attack was directed most specifically toward the discipline as it had been developed (theoretically and methodologically), taught, and used in the last 20 years, during which time it had come to be dominated by behavioral methods and assumptions about the nature of social science and by a commitment to a pluralistic model of the political process in Western societies.

The "behavioral explosion" in political science of the late 1940s and early 1950s turned the discipline away from a traditional (legalistic and historical) approach to the study of politics and introduced a concern (rather late in political science in comparison with other social sciences) for empirical research, operational criteria, and quantification techniques. Most importantly, from the radical point of view behavioralism brought with it a claim to value neutrality—a conviction that social data are themselves neutral, and that employment of the scientific method leads to value-free research results. This claim was most disastrous, from a radical perspective, for its tendency to relieve political scientists of a sense of responsibility for the moral or ideological implications of their research. And ultimately, it came to justify the involvement of political scientists in research and advisory activities for government agencies on the grounds that their work was ideologically neutral regardless of its institutional context, its sources of support, or the uses to which it was put. Rather than tending to remove political scientists from involvement with policy making, then, the value-neutrality principle merely covered the supportive role of political scientists in relation to government and the corporate establishment with "a thin veil of scientificity" (Surkin & Wolfe, 1970, p. 4).

But the major source of a distinctively conservative bias in political science in the last two decades, according to the radical critique, has been the wide acceptance of pluralist theory, which tends to equate elite bargaining and negotiation with the generic concept of politics. In this view any politics that does not take place within the highly controlled context of a legislative committee, executive bureau, and interest-group sub-system, and that is based instead on the mobilization of community tensions through mass participatory structures and ideological appeals, is looked upon as "extremist," "deviant," "irresponsible," or "dysfunctional" (Baskin, 1970, pp. 71–72).

Inherent in the pluralist interpretation of American politics, it is argued, is the conviction that pluralism works, in the sense of granting all groups in the society potential influence in the distribution of political rewards, and that it is, in fact, "the best [system] one could hope for in an imperfect, but not evil, world" (Surkin & Wolfe, 1969, p. 50). Consistent with this positive evaluation of pluralist systems is an acceptance of limited political participation as a source of stability within American democracy and a disinclination toward major change in the existing democratic order.

Dissident political scientists charge the pluralist model with an inability to deal with present upheavals in American society, with a failure to "provide an analysis of the politics of those who are excluded from the interest-group universe and victimized by it," and, most importantly, with reinforcing the system that it purports merely to describe, by teaching "political vocabularies and role orientations resulting in forms of behavior that confirm the appropriateness of its own categories" (Baskin, 1970, p. 72).

The essential compatibility of the behavioral and pluralist perspectives in political science lies in their mutual commitment to model building, in their tendency to promote specialization of research problems and methodological techniques, and in the desire of their proponents to avoid the involvement of their discipline in serious criticism of the American democratic system—because of the behavioralist emphasis on scientific "neutrality," on the one hand, and because of the pluralists' positive assessment of American democracy, on the other.

The association

The role of the APSA in establishing and maintaining the predominance of behavioralism in political science has been described briefly above. Corresponding closely to the rise of behavioral methodology, the pluralist perspective also began during the 1950s to predominate within the discipline and the APSA. Meanwhile, the increasingly national orientation of the profession enhanced the importance of association resources, making the governance of the APSA of vital interest to dissidents who joined CNPS. Participation in decision making regarding the allocation of APSA resources was, they pointed out, extremely limited. Attendance at the annual business meeting—the only forum for membership participation in the official business of the organization—was consistently well below 1 percent of the membership. One candidate for each association office was selected annually by an appointed nominating committee and routinely "elected" at the business meeting. At no point in the history of the association had the official nominee for any APSA office been challenged by a member-sponsored candidate, although provision for such a contest was made in the APSA constitution. And finally, the members of the nominating committee and their nominees alike came—to a disproportionate extent—from high-prestige institutions on the East and West Coasts, had received their doctoral degrees from high-prestige schools, and represented a predominantly behavioral orientation toward the study of political science (Wolfe, 1969). Thus, governance of this influential organization was neither democratic nor representative.

The Proposed Reform

The first objective of the Caucus for a New Political Science —and that which united the greatest number of caucus members—was the creation of a "radical" or critical political science that would address itself to exactly those issues ignored and neglected by a behavioralist-dominated discipline and that would engage in extensive critical examination of existing political and social systems and seek to create radical alternatives to them.

Some caucus members saw the necessity not only for a critique of the pluralist theory, but for the creation, as well, of "new paradigms for research and political analysis of new modes of inquiry . . . to contend with today's social problems, new political subcultures, new modes of human experience and behavior, and so on" (Surkin & Wolfe, 1969, p. 60).

Secondarily, the caucus sought to reform the APSA as an organization: to democratize it, to sever its links with government, and to urge it to devote its resources to encouraging the study of critical social problems. In addition, the caucus's concern with reforming professional institutions and practices extended beyond the APSA to inequities within the broader discipline: to discrimination against blacks, women, foreign born, graduate students—and dissident scholars—and to the failure of the reward system to recognize good teaching as a professional activity at least as meritorious as publication.

An early *Newsletter* of the caucus places these various tasks in a clear order of priority, asserting:

[As] probably all Caucus members would agree, we are *primarily* an *intellectual* revolt, and not primarily an *organizational* one. We may very well engage in organizational revolt, and seek organizational change, but only to facilitate our primary aim. It might be said that we are only *instrumentally* concerned with changing the *organizations* of political science, but we are fundamentally concerned with changing the *study* of political science (The Caucus for a New Political Science, 1968, pp. 4–5, italics in original).

HISTORY OF THE CAUCUS The shifting composition and activities of the caucus as it has pursued its goals can most clearly be seen in terms of three stages of caucus history. We will characterize these as (1) the *early coalition,* which lasted from September 1967 to roughly September 1970; (2) the *political activist* stage, which lasted from the September 1970 convention of the APSA to the September meetings in 1971; and (3) the *radical intellectual* stage, which has lasted from the fall of 1971 to the present.

The Early Coalition: 1967–1970 The membership of CNPS was, from the beginning, predominantly young, and graduate students played a key part in bringing the caucus into existence. Nevertheless, in all but the brief political activist stage of caucus history, the 21-man executive committee of CNPS has consistently included a significant number of older and well-established academicians among its ranks. The mixture of age groups and academic ranks was particularly great during the first $2^1/_2$ years of the caucus's existence, when CNPS represented a "grand coalition" between three different types of dissidents within the political science profession: (1) political scientists specifically concerned with promoting policy studies, (2) traditionalists and political theorists, and (3) a younger group of more politically oriented radicals.

Political theorists and policy-oriented caucus members A significant force in the formation and early activity of the caucus was a group of political theorists or "philosophers" (radical intellectuals) whose alienation from the mainstream of the discipline had its origins in the behavioral revolution and in the processes of professionalization that had transformed political science in the previous two decades. Concerned primarily with intellectual processes within the association and the discipline, this group joined the caucus in its efforts to reintroduce a central concern for traditional ethical-moral issues in the study of politics.

Similar in orientation and style to the political theorists was a group of political scientists (who can be characterized as left-liberal reformers) primarily concerned with devoting the intellectual resources of political science to the critical analysis of contemporary political problems and policies and with urging the APSA to promote and support a wider range of policy studies.

Within these two groups were a considerable number of established professors, a few with formidable reputations in their field. The members of both these groups defined themselves first as intellectuals rather than as political activists and tended to identify more closely with their discipline—both as an intellectual enterprise and as a system of social values and norms—than with groups comprising the New Left. Many of these caucus members had already made an extensive investment in careers in political science (some in serious efforts to change the field), and they were not generally prepared as caucus members to engage in militant confrontations with "establishment" political scientists. Some members of this group believed, moreover, that the establishment was made up of reasonable men whose attention needed only to be turned to the critical issues raised by the caucus—who could, in short, be reformed.

The members of these two groups shared a disinclination to engage their association in direct political action—by committing it, for example, to public stands on controversial political issues, or by devoting association resources to social and political action programs. But they differed importantly in the nature of the reform that they sought *within* the association. On the conservative side, one eminent policy-oriented member of the caucus, Theodore Lowi (whose firm conviction that the APSA should be pressed to become once again a more ideal-type learned society made him virtually unique within the caucus), led the opposition to democratizing, or politicizing, association governance. He argued that it was the inappropriate involvement of a scholarly society such as the APSA in governmental and other external relations that had given impetus to the equally inappropriate movement to politicizing internal leadership processes.

If we severed our Association from its intimate relations with government and the Democratic Party, if we got the Association out of its various exterior service roles . . . if we ceased encouraging political scientists to make the job of policy-making and leadership easier rather than more difficult, if we, in sum, did whatever we could to make the Association independent and to make it serve more as a balance wheel than a cog wheel . . . the officialdom of the Association would no longer be responsible for making decisions that politicize their roles and offices (Lowi, 1969, pp. 276–77).

Successful reform of the APSA would thus consist of reducing organizational involvement in external political affairs, a step that would render the question of who governed the association *less* important rather than more important and would obviate the need for drastic change in the association governance structure.

On the radical end of the continuum was a larger number of political theorists who argued that the inalterable importance of the association in allocating vital resources such as national prestige within the profession made the question of association governance, inescapably, a political one. This group urged the democratization of association governance processes as a necessary step toward reallocating association resources so as to foster and encourage the kind of moral inquiry in political science called for by the crisis in the society. The argument for the necessity for internal politicization and democratization of the APSA became the dominant one within the caucus during its most active years, with the result that the policy-oriented segment of the membership was the first to fall away from active participation in caucus activities.

Radical activist caucus members Also prominently represented on the caucus executive committee was a group of young political activists who tended to feel closely allied to the left movement outside the association. In the words of two of its most articulate spokesmen, Alan Wolfe and Marvin Surkin, this group was made up primarily of:

political scientists who believe that the future of the CNPS movement will depend on a critical evaluation of American institutions and a confrontation with prevailing social injustices—"poverty, racism and imperialism" [and that] what is needed, therefore, is analysis of alternative social priorities, devising models of social change and strategies for political action—action-research projects—and *political* commitment on the part of the intellectual (1969, p. 61, italics in original).

This segment of the caucus characteristically pressed the APSA to adopt resolutions on controversial policy issues such as the war in Vietnam and to devote its resources to political action or action-research programs. This strategy was not officially supported by the caucus (which the radical intellectuals dominated for all but the year 1970–71), but the introduction of such resolutions at the APSA business meetings by young dissidents known to be caucus members and the generally militant behavior of these members at those meetings played an important part in shaping the image of the caucus for the majority of association members.

Early Caucus Strategies and Activities During the first two years of CNPS activity, the executive committee concentrated its major efforts on sponsoring panel sessions and workshops designed to supplement the regular program at the APSA conventions and to make it more relevant to contemporary political problems. APSA officials provided hotel space for these panels and listed them in the predistributed convention program. They regularly attracted overflow audiences and were considered by caucus members to be highly successful in terms of their quality and the intensity of debate they frequently engendered.

These panels received broad support from the various subgroups within the caucus. A few members argued that the panels failed to influence the content of the regular sessions of the conventions, and that it would be more appropriate to send "truth squads" into the meetings at large to challenge the content of the official association program and to debate substantive issues before the wider membership. Truth squads were never mobilized, however. It was generally believed within the caucus that separate panels provided a more coherent format for searching political analysis.

In addition to organizing its own panels, the caucus successfully sponsored a constitutional amendment committing the association to actively encourage "in its membership and its journal, research in and concern for significant contemporary political and social problems and policies, however controversial and subject to partisan discourse in the community at large these may be." The caucus scored a victory, as well, in bringing about the passage of a resolution abolishing the association's awards to congressmen.

In addition, the caucus established four investigative commissions concerned with graduate education, with institutions of the political science profession, with the status of nonwhite personnel, and with the status of women in the profession. The latter two commissions were particularly instrumental in illuminating the discriminatory practices against women and blacks in the profession and gave impetus to the subsequent formation of both the women's and blacks' caucuses within the APSA.

The most dramatic confrontation between the caucus and the APSA establishment occurred during the September 1968 business meeting, which took place in Washington D. C., not long after the Democratic Convention in Chicago. Following the passage of a fairly mild resolution that moved the site of the 1970 APSA convention out of Chicago, caucus members attempted to substitute a more strongly worded resolution that censored Mayor Daley and the Chicago police for their brutal and repressive actions and specified that these actions were the basis for changing the convention site. When a caucus member was ruled out of order and debate on the alternate resolution cut short, caucus members initiated a walkout that eventually attracted 200 people from the business meeting to a countersession in a nearby room, generating much excitement and adding large numbers of new names to the caucus membership list. By the end of the 1968 convention, the caucus boasted 400 dues-paying members.

The experience was a heady one for the newly formed caucus. It suggested that feelings of moral outrage could, indeed, be aroused among large segments of the association membership and that confrontation with APSA leadership could successfully dramatize repressive practices in the governance of the association. This was the moment at which the caucus movement held out the most promise to the broadest range of dissidents within the association. Never again was there as strong a sense of solidarity among the disparate groups that had brought the caucus into existence. The most militant actions at the business meeting were those of caucus activists, but they were widely condoned within the CNPS as a whole because of the prevailing sense of outrage both at the events of the Democratic Convention and at the handling of the association meeting. As a result, it seemed to the left wing of the caucus that CNPS, for all its diversity of membership, would support and engage in militant action, where provoked, and that it was in some sense a legitimately "radical" caucus.

Before the end of the 1968 meetings, however, the caucus confronted its first seriously divisive issue. This began with a proposal that Daniel P. Moynihan and Morris Janowitz be asked to join the CNPS executive committee—a proposal strongly rejected by several activist members of the committee. Moynihan and Janowitz were proposed on the grounds that they were social scientists of eminence who rejected the behavioral claim to value neutrality in social research and who argued the necessity for social scientists to assume responsibility for the critical assessment of social policy. Men of such wide reputation would lend the caucus respectability, it was argued, and thereby enhance its influence on the political science profession.

From the radical perspective, however, these men "symbolized . . . exactly what we formed the Caucus to fight. Not speculative thinkers who were persistent and intelligent critics of liberalism were uncovered, but social scientists who were policy makers and whose policies represented the repressive reality of the America we were disenchanted with" (Wolfe, 1971, p. 395). Nevertheless, Janowitz and Moynihan were elected to the executive committee, to the dismay of at least one caucus activist, Alan Wolfe, who later wrote: "For two years it was a standing joke among radicals in the social sciences that a 'radical' caucus contained those men, a perception which practically precluded co-operation with caucuses in other fields" (ibid., p. 396).

Although Moynihan and Janowitz participated only briefly in caucus affairs, their election, combined with the other events of the 1968 meetings, illustrates a fundamental confusion concerning the nature of CNPS that was to persist through all the various stages of the radical movement in political science: Was the caucus to seek change by confronting the APSA establishment, militantly and aggressively, and by dramatizing its profound differences with, or alienation from, that establishment? Or was it to try to attain respectability within the association, seeking support from men of influence who agreed with some part of its critique and attempting in the manner of a loyal opposition to gain acceptance of its ideas and programs?

The issue had in no way been resolved when the caucus began, in 1969, to run slates of candidates, on a caucus platform, for association office.

The election strategy was initially conceived as a means of widening membership participation in association affairs and of raising controversial issues for debate. At the time this strategy was first proposed, it was still formal procedure for association elections to be held at the annual business meeting and for official nominees to be ratified, without issue, by the small number of members present. In proposing to challenge this tradition, caucus members visualized the transformation of the business meeting into a vital forum in which political scientists might confront each other to debate the issues on which the candidates for election would explicitly state their views. The limitation on the number of members who could participate in such annual meetings (both in terms of the travel costs involved and in terms of the size of a group that could effectively engage in intense debate) was a problem that the caucus never resolved, although it proposed that funds be found to bring people to the meeting who could not otherwise attend, that more time be allotted for the conduct of business, and that business meeting procedures be "adapted to the facts of conflict" (Kettler, 1969*b*, p. 47).

This vision was never realized, however, as a result of a constitutional amendment passed (despite strong caucus opposition) immediately prior to the 1969 election, which provided that all contested elections of officers (as well as all constitutional amendments) be submitted to a mail referendum of the association membership. This amendment was an outgrowth of the fear of a group of liberals within the association that the business meetings would be "packed" by the caucus with local graduate students and others sympathetic to its resolutions and candidates.

With face-to-face debate no longer a likely outcome of contested elections, the strategy lost some of its dramatic appeal for those caucus activists who had seen the elections as a promising form of confrontation with association leadership. And following the first contest in 1969, the drama paled still further for those activists who had devoted time and energy to the campaign—partly because the strategy was no longer new, and partly because the results of the election demonstrated conclusively that there was not a significant number of radicals among the association membership waiting to be mobilized by the caucus. While the CNPS slate averaged one-third of the vote (in the largest vote ever polled in the APSA), only one of its candidates gained a council seat—a "marginal" caucus member originally selected by the APSA nominating committee and endorsed, secondarily, by the CNPS. Following the 1969 election (and each contested election thereafter) a group of activist members of the caucus argued against running further slates—and withdrew from the caucus when they failed to change its commitment to this strategy.

The most continuous support for running slates of candidates came from the dominant group of radical intellectuals and left-liberals within CNPS who saw the elections as both an important "educational device" and as a means of gaining representation for the caucus—however marginal—in APSA offices. This group saw positive signs in the 30 percent vote for caucus-affiliated candidates and began to talk of devising a slate to run in the 1970 election that would increase that percentage. Thus, the caucus candidate for the association presidency in 1970 was Hans Morganthau, an eminent (and controversial) political scientist who strongly opposed the Vietnam War and who seemed to stand a modest chance of actually winning the election. In fact, in a letter to the editor of the *Chronicle of Higher Education* written just prior to the 1970 election, the outgoing chairman of the caucus, David Kettler (a radical intellectual who had been a strong proponent of the election strategy), asserted that the caucus slate "may well win" (1970a, p. 3).

The caucus's disregard for both Morganthau's anticommunism and his generally "realist" views on foreign policy reflected the willingness of the caucus executive committee to compromise ideological "purity" in that election in a serious bid for power within the APSA. When that bid failed, the caucus had lost both credence and momentum. To radical political scientists, the caucus looked like a loyal opposition of very ambiguous ideological persuasion. To one vociferous group of liberals within the association, organized by Donald Herzberg in 1969 to oppose the caucus, the election strategy of the CNPS was a clear attempt to "gain control" of the association and to use its name and resources for partisan political purposes. For several years, this group, which designated itself The Ad Hoc Committee for a Representative Slate, formed its own slate of candidates to oppose the caucus nominees, supporting all the association-endorsed candidates except those drawn by the nominating committee from the CNPS executive committee. In a mimeographed letter to the full membership of the association in 1969 the Ad Hoc Committee warned:

This election will determine whether the Association is to be a professional organization based on shared interests and expertise in scholarship, research, and teaching or whether it is to become a political action group . . . . The Caucus advocates the full-scale politicization of the Association and the use of its resources to advance a political action program (Herzberg, n.d., pp. 1–2, italics in original).

This anticaucus campaign seems to have contributed significantly to the difficulty of getting radical caucus members elected to the APSA council. A number of "moderate" association-endorsed caucus candidates were defeated by Ad Hoc nominees, and many caucus members were convinced that the Ad Hoc Committee's "slanderous" statements concerning the CNPS and its individual members played an important part in shaping the image of the caucus among the association membership at large and prevented it from mobilizing all the support it might have found among political scientists disenchanted with APSA leadership.

**The Political
Activist Stage:
1970–71**

Even before the results of the 1970 elections were known, however, the caucus underwent an abrupt shift in personnel and moved from the East Coast, where it had been strongly centered in New York City, to the West Coast, where its new center of activity was Los Angeles. The APSA convention was held in Los Angeles in 1970, making it difficult for many caucus members from Eastern schools to attend. At the same time, most of the original members of the executive committee were exhausted with the effort that organizing panels and elections had consistently demanded of them and wished to turn their attention to other forms or loci of activity. As it happened, Los Angeles was the center for the only flourishing regional division of the CNPS, the Western Caucus for a New Political Science (WCNPS), and members of this subgroup were present in sufficient numbers at the L.A. convention to take over the reins. That year, 14 out of 21 executive committee posts went to West Coast members, and almost no members were reelected to the committee from the previous year.

Although the new executive committee was made up of political activists to a much larger extent than previously, the strategies of the caucus did not change drastically. Rather, the major preoccupation within the caucus was the question of whether to remain within the APSA at all, and if not, what sort of alternative structure to seek. During the 1970 association meetings, a left group had already disengaged from the CNPS to form the Union of Radical Students of Politics, a group committed to a combination of radical political scholarship and action. By 1971, few scholar-activists remained committed to working within the APSA. When the association met in Chicago in September of that year, the caucus again shifted hands, with a nearly complete turnover in executive committee membership from the previous year and a return to major activity on the East Coast.

**The Radical
Intellectual
Stage: 1971–73**

After the 1971 convention the caucus executive committee was composed almost entirely of radical intellectuals, a very few of whom were instrumental in establishing the caucus originally and in devising its strategies as a counterorganization. The scale of caucus activity was drastically reduced; the executive committee met only irregularly and drew fewer committee members than ever before, and general caucus meetings were attended by strikingly few graduate students or young professors of political science. The major concern of the executive committee was characterized in 1972 as "survival." For the first time, the APSA had ruled to give no support to separate caucus panels at the 1972 convention (to provide no hotel space and to list no caucus panels in the official convention schedule). This action suggested that the APSA no longer viewed the caucus as a distinctive intellectual force within the association. How the decision would affect the future relationship between the weakened caucus and the association was a major question confronting its executive committee.

MINORITY GROUPS IN THE APSA In February of 1969, $1^1/_2$ years after the emergence of the Caucus for a New Political Science, the APSA council established the association Committee on the Status of Blacks in the Profession and the Committee on the Status of Women in the Profession for the purpose of studying the problems of these groups and of improving their position within political science.[1] At the subsequent APSA convention in September 1969, caucuses were convened by women and blacks to support the work of the association committees but to work independently of the formal structure of the APSA, leaving them free to adopt stands and to engage in activities more critical of association leadership and policy than would be possible for official committees. In 1970, a committee and caucus were also created to concern themselves with the status of Chicanos in political science.

Each of these groups asserted the uniqueness of its problems and needs in the profession and bitterly resisted the eventual efforts of the APSA council to consolidate their programs under the jurisdiction of a single Committee on Professional Equality. Nevertheless, the claims that these groups made upon the APSA and the organizational response to their demands are

---

[1] Although women compose a statistical majority in the general population, they are a minority in the APSA and are included in the term *minority* with blacks and Chicanos in the following discussion.

similar in some important respects. All criticized the association for the merely token inclusion of minority groups in its scholarly activities and in its leadership and decried the lack of responsibility assumed by the APSA for ending discrimination against minority groups in the profession. All three groups demanded that the association devote attention and resources to eliminating inequities in the opportunity structure in political science and that it concern itself with the problem of recruiting minority-group members into the field and of providing them with equal employment—a concern that would involve the APSA in a direct attempt to influence university departmental policy.

To an important extent, of course, women, blacks, and Chicanos also sought through their work within the association to raise member consciousness concerning attitudes toward, and treatment of, minority groups in the profession. In this respect their objectives resembled those of the radical caucus, which perceived the association primarily as a vehicle through which to change the perspectives and commitments of political scientists. But more than the CNPS, the minority-group committees and caucuses focused their attention on departmental policy reform and called upon the APSA to exert influence on the patterns of recruitment of students and faculty and on the conditions of employment within the university.

These minority-group demands were presented as resolutions to the APSA council and subsequently to the annual business meeting for membership approval. In their general substance, the resolutions committed the association to:

1 Promote recruitment of minority-group members into the profession.

2 Oppose discrimination in the employment of minority-group members and to employ sanctions against institutions and organizations found to be guilty of discrimination (by public censorship, by denying them use of the APSA employment service, and by the withdrawal of association investments). The APSA was also urged to provide funds for legal counsel for minority-group members seeking to bring charges of discrimination against employers.

3 Provide association fellowships and scholarships and to seek outside funds to support research and graduate work for minority-group members.

4 Assure more adequate representation of minority groups in APSA governance and their more active participation in association meetings.

5 Support black, feminist, and Chicano studies.

In contrast to the issues raised by the Caucus for a New Political Science, these concerns were granted immediate legitimacy by association leadership and membership, as indicated by the creation of formal committees—supported by association funds—to work toward enhancing minority-group status and also by the successful passage of many resolutions sponsored by the three committees.

The original budget allocation to support the work of the Committee on Blacks in 1969–70 was $30,000, representing half of the total allocation to the association's 10 committees in that fiscal year ("Report of the Treasurer . . . ," 1969, p. 562) and demonstrating leadership recognition of the importance and particular severity of the problems of black political scientists. It reflected, as well, a recognition of the more critical financial needs of blacks than of women (whose budget allocation was $4,000 in that year) to improve their status in the discipline.

Although the budget for the women's committee was limited, recognition of the legitimacy of women's claims upon the association was demonstrated by the consistent council and membership approval of their committee resolutions. These resolutions were, on the whole, more easily encompassed within the scholarly and liberal ethos of the APSA than were those of the blacks and Chicanos, partly because the women's committee made more moderate demands upon the association's financial resources and partly because their claims were more consistent with the professional ethos of the association. Women in the profession tend to come from the same socioeconomic background as the men who dominate the field, and they urged reforms that would grant them equal opportunity and rewards for equal professional competence (reforms such as accommodation for part-time graduate work in university departments, the creation of part-time teaching posts, and the abolition of antinepotism rules). Blacks and Chicanos, on the other hand, argued the responsibility of the APSA to make financial compensation for the severe socioeconomic deprivation of their members in the past and for their greater financial handicap in entering the profession in the present, and were continuously dissatisfied with the budget allocations to support their committee programs. In addition, blacks in particular pressed the need for representation of "black interests" (as defined by the Committee on the Status of Blacks) on all association policy bodies and demanded a major role in selecting representatives to such bodies—a demand that was perceived by association leadership as conflicting with the "professional" standards and criteria that had traditionally determined committee appointments and election to association office. Such demands generated greater conflict between blacks (and to a lesser degree Chicanos) and the APSA "establishment" than characterized the relations between women and the association.

The question of monetary support for minority-group committees became particularly explosive in 1970, when the APSA confronted a financial crisis and began to cut back allocations to a number of its committees and programs. [In his annual report for the fiscal year 1968–69, the APSA treasurer blamed inflationary pressures and an expanding range of committee activities for the fact that association expenditures had for two years exceeded income (ibid., p. 592).] The budgetary crisis brought into sharp focus the question of association priorities. Blacks, women, and the newly created Committee on the Status of Chicanos all argued that their programs ought to be granted precedence over older commitments of the association—suggesting, for example, that funds for the journal or for association-sponsored research projects should be cut back or that the APSA endowment fund (of $600,000) should be used to provide generous, ongoing support for minority activities (Klotsburger, 1971; Committee on the Status of Blacks in the Profession, 1970). Blacks in particular argued that the enormity of their problems warranted a drastic revision in association priorities to assure adequate support of their work. When such a shift was not made and the allocation for the Committee on Blacks was reduced, black association members protested by boycotting the 1970 convention. While they were subsequently to resume their committee activities, blacks have since continued to pressure the council for more substantial funding.

All three committees also pressed the association for autonomy in carrying on their work, on the grounds that the needs and interests of each of their groups were unique and required definition by group members themselves. One major issue concerned control over the expenditure of association funds allocated to minority-group committees and the desire of these committees to apply through the APSA for foundation grants to support minority programs and then to assume independent control over the use of such grants. The council argued in opposition that the association could not accept foundation funds without retaining some responsibility for their expenditure. And while the APSA leadership made efforts to expand the independence of the minority-group committees within the limits defined by the council, the committees were never granted the kind of autonomy that they considered essential to their effective functioning.

Ultimately, critical limits on the APSA's response to minority-group demands were established by the council's refusal (1) to cut back or eliminate other major association programs (such as the publication of the *Directory* or of the *APSR*) for the sake of devoting a larger proportion of the budget to minority-committee activities; (2) to grant minority committees significantly more autonomy than was enjoyed by other association committees; (3) to appoint representatives of minority groups to all APSA committees; or (4) to allow minority committees to select their own representatives to major association policy bodies. In each of these respects, the APSA leadership defended the traditional orientation and commitments of the association against the potentially unlimited demands of groups (in this case, blacks and Chicanos) that argued that equalization of opportunity in the profession should now be the *first* obligation of the APSA. Positive actions of the association on behalf of minority groups, however—its public stands promoting participation of disadvantaged groups in the profession, its allocation of funds for committee work and scholarships, and its efforts to increase minority participation in association governance and programs—indicated a willingness to make equalization of opportunity *one* of its ongoing commitments without fundamentally altering organizational procedures or goals or the reward structure that the association serves in the discipline.

IMPACT OF THE CAUCUS MOVEMENT ON THE APSA One of the most explicit effects of dissident activity within the APSA after 1967 was a redistribution of power among the various association bodies and offices that had traditionally been the loci of formal decision making. Prior to 1967, governance of the association was effectively in the hands of a nine-member executive committee of the council, which met three times a year. Its decisions were routinely ratified by the council, which met perfunctorily at the annual convention, and by the poorly attended business meeting. As an immediate consequence of dissident activity in 1967 and 1968, however, the 26-man council began to meet four or five times each year, taking upon itself the responsibility that it had previously vested in the smaller executive committee and, in effect, putting the committee "out of business." Wider participation in the policy process was also effected by the creation of new committees (among them an important Finance Committee and a Program Review and Planning Committee), whose responsibility for advising and informing the council placed them in a position of key importance in the changing governance structure. At the same time, association presidents became much more extensively involved in the governance process (although there was no formal revision of presidential powers), while the role of the executive director shifted to involve him more in the coordination of committee and council activities and less in actual decision-making processes.

The business meeting, previously the final locus of policy decisions, was greatly reduced in formal importance by the constitutional amendment adopted in 1969 that required all contested elections and constitutional amendments to be submitted to a mail referendum. Despite this limitation on its powers, however, the business meeting continued to attract far larger numbers of association members and to generate enough debate over policy issues that several lengthy sessions were scheduled at each convention for the conduct of business.

Of particular importance in promoting wider participation in association governance was the creation of a fairly stable two-party system, the result of the annual challenge to official nominees for association office by CNPS-sponsored slates of candidates. The CNPS slates continue to command a significant proportion of the membership vote; and while no CNPS candidate has been elected APSA president to date, a few caucus members have succeeded in gaining council seats, and a successful bid for the presidency still seems a future possibility.

It is also clear that radical caucus and minority-committee activities have created new awareness of, and concern for, a variety of social issues within the APSA, reflected not only in the passage of many minority-committee resolutions, but also in the abolition of the Congressional Distinguished Service Awards and the more self-conscious attention to the association's investment policy. According to a 1970 council decision, for example, the APSA will in the future "avoid investments inconsistent with the preservation of a democratic and humane social order" ("Report of the Treasurer . . . ," 1970, p. 592).

Finally, members of CNPS and association leadership agree that significantly more attention is being devoted within the APSA to political and social issues of contemporary importance. This change in intellectual focus is most conspicuously absent in the content of the *APSR*, whose editorial policy still reflects a strong commitment to behavioral research. A new dedication to critical social analysis and a reawakened concern for normative issues within political science have gained expression, rather, through publication channels outside the association. Radical political scientists have created their own journal, *Politics and Society*, to provide an outlet for work dealing with current political issues.

Nevertheless, despite the recent association policy to discontinue sponsorship of separate panels organized by groups such as the CNPS, there has been a noticeable effort to incorporate topics of interest to the caucus, as well as participation of caucus members themselves, in the formal association program, reflecting the concern of the membership as a whole with the questions raised by this group. To this extent, association meetings have been "opened up" and the scholarly reward system touched, if not dramatically altered, by the dissident activity of the late 1960s and early 1970s.

5. The Radical Challenge in the Modern Language Association of America

The Modern Language Association of America (MLA) was founded in 1883 "to promote study, criticism and research in modern languages and their literatures, and to further the common interests of teachers of these subjects." By 1968, its membership (composed predominantly of college teachers of English literature and foreign languages) had reached nearly 30,000; it had acquired a headquarters staff of nearly 70, and was operating on an expense budget of over a million dollars, not including the grants and contracts that partially supported the association's ongoing projects ("Report of the Executive Secretary," 1969).

The primary preoccupation of the MLA—manifest in the focus of its annual meetings and in the content of its journal, *Publications of the Modern Language Association of America (PMLA)*—has consistently been scholarship. In keeping with this concern, the association has carried on a number of projects designed to promote and facilitate literary and linguistic studies, among them a computerized international bibliography, a computerized abstract system, and a major publication program to make available texts of works by classical American writers.

More peripheral to the concerns of the majority of MLA members and to the reward structure in the association and the profession, but involving extensive adminstrative effort and substantial government and foundation support, have been the MLA projects to improve teaching of English and foreign languages in American high schools. The association's foreign language program was initiated in 1952 (with support from the Rockefeller Foundation) in an effort to "discover the proper role of foreign language learning in the U. S., to dramatize the results of this investigation to the public, and to improve the tools, the methodology, and the personnel for language teaching" (Fisher, 1969, p. 24). This program is credited with having played an important part in bringing about the inclusion of foreign languages in the National Defense Education Act of 1958 and with having increased high school enrollments in foreign languages between 1948 and 1965 (ibid.). Supported since 1968 by the U. S. Office of Education, the foreign language program continues to occupy the time of a substantial proportion of the MLA headquarters staff.

Of more recent origin is the association's cooperative English program of the last decade through which the association contributed to the development of "Project English" of the U. S. Office of Education and devoted extensive effort to distributing experimental curricular material to English Institutes funded by the National Defense Education Act.

These projects elicited over $300,000 in government and foundation grants and contracts in 1967, about half of the total amount received in grants and contracts by the MLA that year ("Report of the Trustees and of the Treasurer," 1968, p. 545). But while annual reports of the MLA executive secretary consistently devote generous attention to this support and to the association's involvement in and commitment to programs related to teaching, only a small percentage of association members take an active interest in these teaching programs. These programs also seem to have had little success in generating wide faculty interest in teacher training. For example, there has been strikingly meager support within college and university English departments for summer institutes (that the MLA helped initiate) directed toward the improvement of high school English teaching (Ohmann, 1969, p. 334).

In fact, recognizing that the profession of language teachers was "not identical with that of linguistic and literary scholars [and] should, ideally, be centered in the schools, not the colleges" (Fisher, 1969, p. 24), the MLA supported the creation of a separate organization in 1967 (The American Council on the Teaching of Foreign Languages) to bring together those in the field with a specific interest in the teaching of foreign languages at all levels.

THE MLA AND THE "PROFESSION" A former executive secretary of the MLA has written that "to the extent that there is an identifiable community of college teachers of English and the modern foreign languages in the United States and Canada, it is the membership of the MLA" (ibid., p. 25). Despite the association's commitment to promoting "professionalism" among its diverse members, however, it is difficult to define the profession that it represents, since there is little theoretical or methodological unity to what scholars in English and the foreign languages do. They engage in "literary criticism, literary history, phonology, semantics, biography, bibliography, editing, poetics, cultural criticism, curricular planning, etc.—and also teaching. There is no common core of knowledge, no 'discipline,' no theoretical framework, no central pragmatic problem to be solved" (Ohmann, 1969, p. 338).

As a result of the intellectual pluralism to which it is, by nature, committed, the MLA cannot be characterized as standing for a central direction in literary and linguistic studies any more specific than the promotion of "detached" or "professional" scholarship. The MLA could not, for example, wield the kind of influence on work done in the study of languages and literature that the APSA has wielded—through its promotion of behavioral methods and pluralist theory—on the study of politics.

The same point can be made more specifically with regard to the association's journal, *PMLA*. While described by one critic as a "standard-setter throughout the profession" (Hux, 1973, p. 54), *PMLA* is noted for its eclecticism more than for its preference for any one school of literary criticism or brand of scholarship. And while there is no denying the prestige within the literary and linguistic fields of having published in *PMLA*, other journals published independently of the MLA (for example, the *Antioch Review* or the *New York Review of Books*) offer equal —and in some circles, even greater—status in the academic world. In this respect, *PMLA* differs strikingly from the *American Political Science Review*, which has long towered over all competitors in its impact on professional status and career advancement in political science. The *APSR* has clearly played a more central role in defining what kinds of work receive prominent recognition in its field.

THE RADICAL CAUCUS Several weeks prior to the December 1968 convention of the MLA in New York City, a group of MLA members within the New University Conference (NUC) ran a letter in the *New York Review of Books* announcing a meeting at Columbia University to plan some tactics for "stirring things up a bit" at the forthcoming convention. According to an NUC leaflet subsequently distributed at the MLA meetings, it was the intention of this group to "raise questions about the response (and responsibility) of our profession to the demands of a society—and a university—in need of radical social change. As a long-range goal, some of us would like to consider the creation of a countermovement or 'radical caucus' within the MLA (or outside of it, if necessary)" (Smith, 1969, p. 344).

The Columbia meeting took place the night before the opening of the MLA convention and attracted more than 500 participants. What generated such wide interest in the creation of a "countermovement" was a combination of concern over the Vietnam War and outrage at the events surrounding the Democratic Convention in Chicago a few months earlier. In response to the "siege of Chicago," the MLA had mailed out a ballot to its members, who voted decisively in favor of meeting in Chicago as scheduled in 1969. It was one aim of the NUC-MLA dissidents to contest this decision at the association's forthcoming business meeting.

However, the most noteworthy events of the 1968 convention were neither planned nor anticipated by NUC members and their supporters. On the first day of the meetings, Louis Kampf, a professor of literature at MIT and an NUC member, and two graduate students were arrested in the lobby of one of the convention hotels. They had scuffled with hotel security guards over some posters that they had put up on the lobby walls protesting the Vietnam War and calling for the "liberation of literature." The arrest was a surprise and a shock to dissidents and MLA leadership alike, and its consequences were more unexpected. At the business meeting two days later, Professor Kampf was nominated from the floor for the second vice-presidency of the association and defeated the official candidate of the nominating committee by a floor vote of 292 to 187. (Voting records from that meeting indicate that at least 550 association members attended, a sharp contrast to the scanty attendance of the year before, when MLA officials, as usual, had difficulty in gathering the quorum of 50 members.) It was the first time in many decades that a candidate nominated from the floor had won election to an MLA office.

Further acts of the 1968 business meeting also reflect the preponderance of support at that meeting for the newly formed radical caucus. Resolutions were passed that condemned the withholding of fellowship funds and loans from college students who engaged in disruptive activities; condemned United States involvement in the Vietnam War; and called upon the United States government to end the draft and upon educational institutions to refuse to cooperate with the Selective Service System. The only "radical" resolution that did not pass called for the abolition of the MLA's Center for American Editions.

In addition, several motions sponsored by the radical caucus passed as "the sense of the meeting," including a motion that the 1969 convention be moved out of Chicago (based on the argument that the wording of the ballot previously distributed to the membership had biased the vote on this issue) and a motion that a committee be established to investigate the situation of women in the profession and to take steps to rectify inequities in their status ("Actions of the 1968 Business Meeting," 1969).

The events of the meeting left even Professor Kampf "flabbergasted" (Scully, 1969, p. 5) and inspired a petition, signed by several hundred association members, expressing indignation that the proportionately small voting majority at the business meeting (roughly 300 out of a total membership of 30,000) could commit the association to political stands and asking the executive council to do whatever possible to invalidate the actions of that meeting. Ultimately, the resolutions were submitted to the wider membership for an "expression of opinion," with the result that all four resolutions passed again, this time with over a third of the membership (about 12,000 people) participating in the vote.

THE RADICAL CRITIQUE

The discipline

While the radical caucus that convened in the MLA in 1968 was eventually to refer to itself as the Radical Caucus in English and the Modern Languages, its NUC leadership and larger membership was composed predominantly of professors of English literature, whose critique of their discipline focused on the nature and development of literary criticism in the United States. During the period following World War II, the literary scene had been significantly transformed by the rise of the New Criticism (or "formalism"), which usurped the position held by literary history as the major preoccupation in academic departments of English, attracting the largest numbers of graduate students and drawing the strongest consideration in curricular and budgetary decision making. Despite its predominance, however, the New Criticism did not completely overshadow or discredit other approaches to the study of literature (such as philology, literary history, or more recent critical approaches such as psychoanalytic criticism). Rather, it contributed to a widening intellectual pluralism that was economically sustained within the academic enterprise by the rapid growth of English departments and the general prosperity of the profession in the postwar period. It is not a major thesis of the radical movement, therefore, that the study of English literature has come to be unduly dominated by one intellectual style or approach in recent decades, or that the hegemony of any one school can be held responsible for the inadequacies of American literary scholarship. Rather, it is argued that the New Criticism shares with earlier schools of criticism and with its present competitors certain assumptions about the relationship between literature and society, and that the doctrinal battles that have preoccupied the literary profession in the United States in recent decades are relatively superficial when viewed against the similarity of all existing schools of criticism in their definitions of the nature and function of literature and the role of the literary scholar in twentieth-century America.

It is the view of the radical left that all major schools of criticism have erred fundamentally in their failure to grant significance to the social context in which literary works are produced and to the relationship of those works to the social lives of those who read them. All schools have tended to define the value of literature (and of literary study) in terms of its contribution to the enrichment of individual lives rather than in terms of its relation to political and social structures, accepting the broader conception of art as a means of individual transcendence of the social world rather than as an instrument for altering consciousness about social and political realities. Within this ideological framework, literary scholars have seen themselves as the preservers and transmitters of literary culture, with a professional obligation to defend their cultural heritage "against science, against politics, against commercialization, against vulgarity, against nearly the whole social process" (Ohmann, 1970,

p. 153). Literature is thus conceived as the property of an intellectual elite, whose professional privilege and whose ensconcement in bourgeois educational institutions was justified by the assumption that the preservation of culture, in itself, served the general good.

The rise to prominence of the New Criticism is not alone responsible for the failures of literary criticism or for the ideological framework within which the academic literary profession has developed in recent decades. But the close attention of the New Criticism to literary texts as isolated entities existing in and for themselves—its close attention to form, to symbolism, to tone in each individual work—represented an explicit attempt "to shut out from consciousness one's own life-situation while reading the poem, and to pry the words loose from their social origins" (ibid., p. 135), an approach clearly compatible with the tendency toward social detachment in the literary profession as a whole. And so, from the perspective of its radical critics, this method has provided natural reinforcement for the "bourgeois" ideology of the literary intellectual in the postwar decades.

From the perspective of the left, one major ramification of this ideology in a period of mass higher education has been the "sterilization" of literature as it is taught to increasingly large numbers of college students. Stripped of any relevance to students' personal lives and experiences, "poems, novels, plays are turned into so many museum pieces students acquire to paint an upper-middle-class patina on their lives" (Cantarow, 1972, p. 60). Literature, as taught in academic departments, is an instrument of social elitism, "enriching" the lives of college students only insofar as it has lifted them out of lower-middle-class and middle-class social strata and provided them (at best) with an escape from the drudgeries of their everyday lives in an oppressive, capitalistic system. For a great many students, however, the study of literature has itself been a form of drudgery, an alienating experience, and, for those who do not succeed in achieving certification through academic programs, a further form of social oppression (Kampf, 1970).

The association

The radical critique of the Modern Language Association differs significantly from the organizational critique articulated by the

Caucus for a New Political Science. To some extent, at least, the divergence in these perspectives reflects major differences between the MLA and the APSA as disciplinary associations. With nearly twice the membership of the APSA (roughly 30,000 members in the late 1960s, compared to the APSA's 17,400) and with a far more elaborate administrative structure, the MLA is seen by its critics as a cumbersome, impersonal, and procedure-ridden bureaucracy, dedicated above all to the efficient administration of its diverse projects and of the affairs of the profession in general. At the same time, the MLA is credited with influencing the scholarship of its members, although in a less specific direction than is the APSA. Despite the fact that it cannot be said to have promoted a particular direction in the theoretical and methodological development of the diverse fields it represents, the MLA is accused of having imposed homogeneity on the work of literary and linguistic scholars through its insistence upon political neutrality and detachment as an essential quality of professional or scholarly work. It is this broad ideological influence on the work being done in their profession that radicals in the MLA most vociferously decry.

At the same time, radicals in the MLA—like their counterparts in other disciplines—accuse their association of "inadvertent" politics, pointing to the MLA's active promotion of professional interests in Washington (for example, its lobbying for the National Endowment for the Humanities) and its generous expenditure of funds and staff time on teaching programs of exclusive benefit to members of the middle and upper classes (Ohmann, 1968a). In investing in such programs, it is argued, the MLA has explicitly attempted to link its own interests with the national interest and has implicity provided support for the status quo.

Also reflecting the concerns of radicals in other fields, dissidents in the MLA have condemned the meritocracy of scholarship prevailing in their association and the oligarchic governance structure through which it finds expression. One critic has pointed out:

In the last thirty-seven years, the MLA has been governed by only about 200 people—officers and members of the Executive Council. More than half of these were on the faculties of Yale, Harvard, NYU, California, Columbia, Princeton, Chicago, Johns Hopkins, and Cornell. The chances of an excellent teacher from the University of Tulsa helping to govern the MLA are negligible; those of a cultural and political activist from Metropolitan Junior College in Kansas City are nugatory. (And of course graduate students and junior faculty are also excluded —Ohmann, 1969, p. 335.)[1]

Strongly supporting this elitist tradition was the unquestioned authority of a nominating committee of eminent scholars who annually proposed one candidate for each elective association office and whose nominees had not been successfully challenged by a member-sponsored candidate in more than half a century.

Finally, women active in the radical caucus were the first to draw attention to the vast discrepancy between the large proportion of female association members (women constituted over one-third of the membership in 1970) and the very small number who had participated in the governance of the MLA.

The Proposed Reform

The most explicit radical alternative to the New Criticism and to the professional ideology it has promoted has been Marxist criticism, an approach to literary analysis that has its origins in the writings of Marx and Engels on the relationship between art and social action. Having enjoyed a brief vogue in American literary circles in the 1920s and 1930s, Marxist criticism was discredited during the cold war period along with Marxism generally and reemerged as a result of the events of the 1960s to receive wider attention than ever before among literary scholars. [A Marxist forum at the 1972 meetings of the MLA attracted several hundred listeners, and an entire issue of *College English* (1972), an official journal of the National Council of Teachers of English, was recently devoted to Marxist literary analysis.]

In contrast to the New Critics' preoccupation with form, Marxist critics are guided by a sociological concern for the *content* of literary art, focusing upon the relationship of works of literature to the social context in which they were written and upon the meaning of such works in the specific historical and social context in which they are read. More specifically, by reawakening the awareness that "writers are concerned with class, race, and sexism...with oppression and liberation" (Wasson, 1972, p. 171) and by focusing new attention on

[1]Copyright © 1969 by the Antioch Review, Inc. First published in the *Antioch Review*, vol. 29, no. 3. Reprinted by permission of the editors.

previously neglected works by and about members of the working class and other oppressed groups, Marxists seek to revitalize literary criticism by enhancing its relevance to the social realities of the present decade, thus building a bridge between their work as writers and teachers and their commitment to social action. Ultimately, one Marxist critic asserts, "Marxists analyze things to be able to act" (Shor, 1972, p. 175).

While not all members of the radical caucus within the MLA accept the designation "Marxist critic" (and many are leery, if not disdainful, of what they label "dogmatic Marxism"), the premises of Marxist analysis are widely accepted by caucus radicals: the need for attention to social content—to class, racism, and sexism—as a basis for a reinvigorated literary criticism; the necessity for integrating literary scholarship and social action; and the importance of teaching literature in such a way as to raise social consciousness and explicitly to counteract bourgeois or "ruling class" ideologies. There have been innumerable disputes among caucus members, of course, concerning interpretations of Marx and, more profoundly, concerning the usefulness of an explicitly Marxian perspective as a basis for radical scholarship, radical teaching, or social action in the 1960s and 1970s. However, the most specific issue that seems to have seriously divided caucus members has been the question of the most appropriate role of the radical literary scholar as social activist.

Uniformly committed to a revolutionary socialist movement in American society—particularly in the late 1960s, when "the movement" still seemed a tangible force in American political life—caucus members disagreed on the appropriate locus for radical action that would support that movement. A minority argued the importance of participating in community-based activity and in other forms of direct political action, convinced that work outside of the academic context was more critical to the achievement of social change than any contribution that might be made through campus-based action. Although this commitment led some radicals to leave academic positions and prompted others seriously to question the efficacy of radical activity within the MLA, adherents of direct political involvement have remained a vociferous minority in the radical caucus into the 1970s.

Caucus leadership and the majority of the membership, on

the other hand, have consistently been composed of scholar-activists who define their central role as that of "oncampus organizers" and radical teachers, arguing that they can best serve the movement through their work in academic institutions. The role of the campus-based activist is admittedly a "fragile" and uncomfortable one, in that the radical daily confronts pressures to conform to academic norms and is constantly in danger of losing his academic post at the same time that he risks losing touch with the revolutionary work being done in the field. But where the contradictions inherent in this role can be tolerated, campus work provides activists the opportunity to organize faculty unions, to radicalize students, to engage in research of use to organizers in the field, and to effect change in academic institutions themselves—for example, through revisions in curriculum and through the introduction of more democratic procedures into the classroom (Lauter, 1969).

It was the dedication to campus-based activism, then, that most heavily influenced the radical challenge to the traditional character of the MLA. Dubious from the start about the possibility of drastically changing or restructuring their association, most caucus members saw MLA meetings as an important context in which to reach and influence other members of their profession. One NUC publication asserted that in the MLA

what is important is the membership. Radicals want to get to people in the MLA—because people are what count, because teachers of language and literature have great impact through their work on the acculturation of young people and on the nature of the school and university system, and because radicals see serious politics inhering in the effort to change people's beliefs and actions, not in parliamentary maneuvering or elitist power plays. Radicals want to change the way teachers see their roles and their work, so they are glad for a chance to use MLA as forums...since what they are after is a redefinition of the profession and a rededication of our professional lives (Ohmann, 1968*b*, p. 7).

As a means to this end, the caucus hoped to introduce political discussion and a critical examination of their profession and its institutions into the meetings of the MLA. They also sought to involve larger numbers and a greater diversity of members in the governance of the association in order to gain expression for previously unrepresented political and professional views and interests.

As indicated in the statement quoted above, it was not a major objective of the Modern Language Caucus in the NUC to "take over" the MLA or even to build a strong power base in the association through concerted political action. The posture of this group consistently shaped the character and strategies of the radical caucus in the MLA—not only because NUC members constituted a substantial and persistent nucleus of the caucus, but because many critical discussions of caucus policy took place at the annual summer meetings of the NUC. For several years after 1968, a full day was set aside at the NUC conventions for NUC-MLA members to discuss caucus strategies and goals. Caucus meetings at the December MLA conventions were thus heavily influenced by the perspectives and commitments of the NUC members who had met together earlier in the year. And since this segment of the caucus felt its strongest organizational base to be outside of the MLA (and sought, among other things, to recruit members of their profession into the NUC), it is not surprising that their objectives with regard to their association differed from those of the Caucus for a New Political Science, which had no direct ties with activist or new left organizations outside the discipline and which explicitly sought to create for itself a base of influence within the APSA. While CNPS developed a consistent program of electoral politics, the radical caucus in the MLA did not.

A significant difference between the two caucuses, in this respect, is that the Radical Caucus in English and the Modern Languages succeeded at its very inception (and almost by accident) in electing one of its members to a key association office, while CNPS devoted a substantial part of its time and energy over a number of years to achieving that end. Kampf's immediate election to the second vice-presidency meant, on the one hand, that during the period of the most intense caucus activity in the MLA, caucus interests were being represented in the very centers of association decision making. On the other hand, Kampf's experience as an officer of the MLA clearly demonstrated that the potential influence of the association's president and vice-presidents was severely limited by the authority of the executive council and (while it still existed) by the business meeting. One analyst of Kampf's vice-presidency pointed out that an association officer whose ideological and organizational commitments reflect dominant trends in the association can play a very important role in initiating new policies and programs, but that an officer whose views and perspectives diverge significantly from those of the majority of the council and of the voting membership at the business meeting is likely to have far less impact (Interview with Francis Lee Utley, 1970). Thus, while Kampf was able (particularly as second vice-president) to initiate change in one area where it was widely agreed that change was needed—in the structure and content of the annual meeting—it is indicative of his limited influence that the major constitutional revisions enacted during his three years in office were all changes to which he and his radical constituency were strongly opposed.

Perhaps because of the obvious limitations on the effectiveness of dissidents elected to association office, but also in keeping with the predominant objectives of the radical caucus, dissidents made no persistent effort to gain key association posts. The radical caucus did join with the Women's Caucus for the Modern Languages in 1970 to run the petition candidate Florence Howe—who was also active in the NUC and a founding member of the radical caucus—for the second vice-presidency. The caucuses were again successful in winning this office. In this instance, the platform on which their candidate ran was more explicitly feminist than radical, and membership support for the objectives of the women's movement in the MLA must be counted as the most significant force behind her election.

When a 232-member delegate assembly was created in 1970 to replace the MLA business meeting, radical caucus members also ran for seats on this body and supported the candidacy of women's caucus representatives as well as of minority-group representatives. By 1972, it was estimated that about 12 people then serving as delegates identified with the radical caucus.

The most consistent efforts of the radical caucus were devoted to the operation of an extensive literature table and to the organization of special sessions at the annual meeting. One immediate result of the radical activity in 1968 was the reorganization of the annual meeting (in which Kampf, as second vice-president, played an important part) to include a considerable number of seminars and workshops on the relationship between politics, the MLA, and the profession; on the economics of the profession; and on the functioning of university departments of language and literature. Small, informal sessions for the discussion of such topics were designed to allow for greater flexibility and spontaneity and for more personal interchange among participants than was possible in the large panel sessions characteristic of MLA meetings. The success of these more intimate seminars and workshops was to make them a permanent part of the format for scholarly meetings as well as for discussions sponsored by the caucus at future MLA conventions. The number of sessions devoted specifically to politics and the profession diminished somewhat in the years following 1969 and 1970, but a major forum on Marxist criticism at the 1972 meetings (which attracted 500 people to an initial paper session) demonstrated both the continued intention of the caucus to generate discussion of the relationship between social and political issues and the study of literature and the continued interest of a significant number of MLA members in participating in such discussion.

The radical caucus was less successful, however, in committing the MLA to public stands on political issues after its initial success in this area in 1968. A resolution opposing the Vietnam War was referred to the membership in 1969 for vote by mail ballot and was defeated. At the same time, association members approved a resolution against committing "the language profession to any position on [current] issues unless they are directly connected with the promotion of literary or linguistic scholarship or are necessary to preserve professional integrity" ("Ballot on Resolutions," 1970). A radical caucus motion that the MLA endorse a People's Peace Treaty with the people of Vietnam was also rejected by a mail-ballot vote in 1971.

Nor did the caucus succeed in promoting the kind of direct member involvement in the governance of the MLA that it had defined as essential to the democratization of the association. While the issues raised at the 1968 meetings directed the attention of association leadership to problems of representation in MLA governance, the resulting constitutional revisions were directly antithetical to the purposes of the caucus. In 1969, the business meeting passed an amendment to the association bylaws requiring that future elections of officers and council members be conducted by mail ballot of the entire membership (rather than by floor vote at the meeting). And in 1970, the business meeting was entirely abolished with the creation of the 232-member delegate assembly, while a mail ballot was required for approval of amendments to the constitution and bylaws as well as of resolutions.

Like their counterparts in the APSA, the radical caucus in the MLA strongly opposed reducing the power of the business meeting, arguing that only in this setting did the membership of the association have the opportunity to engage in face-to-face debate of critical policy issues and, at the same time, to play a formal role in association governance. The mail ballot, it was argued, diminished the effectiveness of the business meeting as an arena in which candidates for office could be called upon to articulate their positions on vital issues, thus raising member awareness of the issues, themselves, and enhancing the possibility that criteria other than scholarly eminence would come to play a significant part in the selection process. Members voting by mail ballot were likely to remain uninformed about the new questions being raised by the radical caucus and other dissident groups in the association, and were prone, therefore, to continue to vote for candidates whose names were widely recognized on the basis of their scholarly work. Under these conditions, petition candidates for office stood a poor chance of defeating the official candidates put forth by the nominating committee.

The official statement defending mail-ballot elections stressed the unlikelihood of a significant proportion of the association membership gathering at the business meeting to participate in a floor vote and the difficulty of transacting business there if large numbers did attend ("Secretary's Elucidation," 1969). For the radical caucus, however, the issue centered on the importance of *direct* member involvement in the governance process. The caucus asserted that the conduct of more important business at the meeting would begin to attract larger attendance and that any resulting disorder in the proceedings would not, in any case, prevent meaningful action there. "Organizational democracy," Kampf declared, "should be more important than running a neat show" ("Observations by Louis Kampf," 1969, p. 3).

For these reasons, the caucus campaigned vigorously against

the introduction of the mail ballot and, subsequently, against the substitution of a delegate assembly for the annual business meeting.

Conceived by a special MLA study commission to assure more systematic representation of member interests in association governance, the delegate assembly was designed to include regional delegates, representatives of the various fields of study within the MLA, and spokesmen, as well, for the "various other constituencies in the association (women, minorities, two-year colleges, and the like)" (*Constitution and Bylaws of the MLA as Revised in December 1970*), all to be elected by the entire membership. However, since the laws under which the MLA was incorporated required that the association be governed only by a board of directors (the executive council) responsible to the entire membership, the executive council was legally constrained from granting formal authority to the delegate assembly as a representative body. The assembly was thus charged with the responsibility for making "recommendations to the executive council with regard to the policies of the association, its direction, its goals and its structure." The result, radical caucus members protested, was simply to enhance the power of the executive council. Where the actions of the council had at least been subject to the formal approval of the membership voting in the business meeting, the substitution of the delegate assembly for the business meeting removed even this restraint, leaving the membership with an "impotent" body through which to express its will (Kampf & Howe, 1971). The adoption of the delegate assembly by the business meeting in 1970, despite its obvious flaws as an instrument of more democratic government, clearly demonstrated the lack of influence of the radical caucus on the direction of the organizational change that its own activities had set in motion.

THE RADICAL CAUCUS MOVES OUT By 1972, following the demise of the NUC, the radical caucus had begun to establish a new, although still informal base of operation outside the MLA, with unofficial headquarters at Wesleyan University. Here East Coast–based members of the caucus (among them a number of the original members of the Modern Language Caucus of the NUC who had founded the radical caucus in the MLA) met several times during the year not only to consider future strategies relating to the MLA, but also to organize independent conferences on themes relating to radical scholarship, teaching, and action. There was a broad sense among participants in these meetings of the need for new and more effective channels of communication among radicals attempting to carry on their work under the increasingly "precarious and demoralizing" conditions in which they found themselves in the university (Harold, 1973). To this end, Wesleyan-based caucus members began to publish a newsletter for distribution to the larger membership, encouraging the radical caucus to begin to "act more like an organization and less like a semispontaneous happening" ("Reports on the MLA," 1973, p. 1) and to focus more on the immediate problems and interests of radical scholars and teachers than on efforts to reform the MLA.

Nevertheless, discussions at Wesleyan and suggestions in the caucus *Newsletter* also indicated plans to meet regularly at the MLA convention, to organize demonstrations and to promote the distribution of radical publications through the operation of a literature table at the meetings, to formulate resolutions to present to the delegate assembly, and to organize panels and workshops on topics of interest to radical scholars of English and the modern languages.

IMPACT OF THE RADICAL CAUCUS ON THE MLA

When asked to assess the impact of the radical caucus on the MLA in the years following 1968, caucus members refer with satisfaction to the dramatic success of the women's movement in the association. The caucus initiated the creation of the Commission on the Status of Women in the Profession (approved by the executive council in 1969) and strongly supported the efforts of women to improve their position in the association and in the profession as a whole.

An important factor in the relationship between the radical caucus and the women's caucus was that the leadership of these groups had a common base in the NUC and shared many political as well as professional objectives. Nevertheless, the women's movement enjoyed a far wider base of support in the MLA (women comprised one-third of the membership in 1972) than did the radical caucus. In addition to membership approval of a broad range of resolutions opposing discrimination against women in the profession and a burgeoning number of sessions devoted to feminist topics at the annual meetings, the impact of the women's movement is apparent in the fact that between 1968 and 1972, every woman officially placed on the ballot for a position on the executive council won election, with the result that there were eight women and seven men on the council in 1973. Only eight women altogether had served on this body in the first 78 years of the association's history (Commission on the Status of Women in the Profession, 1971). In 1973, a dedicated feminist also assumed the presidency of the association (the third woman to hold that office), while women made up one-third of the membership of the delegate assembly.

Members of the radical caucus were also instrumental at the 1969 convention in organizing a Job Seekers Caucus, composed primarily of new Ph.D.'s confronting the declining job market in the language and literature profession. The job caucus attracted wide attendance at its meetings (between 300 and 400 at its initial sessions) and succeeded in turning executive council attention to the inadequacy of the MLA's faculty exchange procedures, which were subsequently revised. Its actions also led to the creation of a Job Market Commission, assigned for one year to study the problems confronted by association members seeking employment, and to the eventual appointment of a permanent Advisory Committee on the Job Market. While the executive council was increasingly sympathetic and responsive to the plight of young graduates in the early 1970s, the demands of the job caucus put into sharp relief the inadequacy of the resources of a disciplinary association such as the MLA for exerting significant influence on the numbers of graduate students put into the job market by college and university departments or for providing real assistance to its graduate student members in their difficult search for employment.

Radical caucus members who had helped to organize job seekers were quickly disillusioned with the possible rewards of serving this constituency. Ambivalent from the start about organizing association members for the achievement of economic goals, they soon became convinced that their work with the Job Seekers Caucus could not be justified as an effort to raise consciousness concerning broader political issues, since those job seekers who managed to find employment rapidly fell away from the caucus. As a result, few radicals showed interest in this movement by 1972.

As described above, the major change in the governance

structure of the MLA that resulted from radical caucus activity was one that radicals, themselves, vigorously opposed— namely, the replacement of the business meeting in 1970 by the delegate assembly, which now makes "recommendations" to the executive council. Although conceived as a means of providing representation to a wide range of groups and interests within the association, the delegate assembly has failed— perhaps in part because it lacks significant formal power as a policy-making body—to command intense interest on the part of either the wider membership of the association or of its own delegates. In an open letter to the MLA membership, the 1973 president reported that fewer than one-third of the association's members had bothered to vote in 1972 for delegates to the assembly and, more significantly, that only two-thirds of the elected delegates had attended the one scheduled meeting of the assembly at the December convention. In fact, long before the end of that meeting, attendance had dwindled to roughly one-third of the full complement of delegates. In addition, during its first two years in existence the assembly did not make clear from its actions whether it was likely to assume the role of a rubber stamp of the executive council or to take some initiative as an independent advisory body (Howe, 1973). As a result, serious questions remained of whether this body would fulfill its intended function of promoting the consistent and significant participation of a wider range of MLA members in association governance.

If the efforts of the radical caucus to democratize and politicize MLA governance processes met with limited success, caucus activity can nevertheless be given a major part of the credit for having produced striking changes in the content of the annual meeting, which continued in 1972 to include discussions of a broad spectrum of political and professional issues once defined as lying entirely outside of the range of appropriate concerns of the MLA. A great deal of impetus for this change has also come, of course, from the organization and activity of women and of job seekers, who have vigorously promoted critical examination of the institutional setting of their profession and particularly of patterns of employment in college and university departments. The problems of these two groups have received even more generous attention at meetings of the MLA than in many other learned societies, no doubt because of the particularly large number of women and of young Ph.D.'s seeking employment among the MLA membership. (The impact of the academic recession on the language and literature fields is discussed in Chapter 7.) On the other hand, the proportionately small number of blacks and other minority-group members who teach English or the modern languages in American colleges and universities accounts for the absence of a black caucus or of other ethnic-group caucuses within the MLA and for the peripheral attention given by the association to the problems of minority groups in the profession. Nevertheless, blacks and Chicanos are explicitly included among the interest groups to be granted regular representation on the delegate assembly, and their interests are being explored and articulated, as well, by an MLA Commission on Minority Groups and the Study of Language and Literature, established in 1973.

Finally, the issues raised by the radical caucus have had a noticeable effect in the heightened concern of association leadership for seeking ways to counteract the cumbersome size and impersonality of the MLA and to reduce the alienation from association affairs felt by a large proportion of its heterogeneous membership. One step in this direction was the introduction of the *MLA Newsletter* in 1969 ("Why an MLA Newsletter?", 1969). In addition, continuous attempts have been made since 1968 to restructure the association's annual convention in such a way as to compensate for its awkward size and complexity and to accommodate both the common and specialized interests of MLA members. A massive membership survey was undertaken in 1973 to determine exactly what those interests are. It remains to be seen whether these efforts will increase member satisfaction with the activities of the association.

6. Liberal Reform in the American Physical Society

Founded in 1899 to promote the "advancement and diffusion of the knowledge of physics," the American Physical Society (APS) has dedicated its attention and resources almost exclusively to the organization of scientific meetings and the publication of journals. Its publication program alone consumed over $3 million of the society's $3½ million expense budget in 1971 ("1971 APS Finances," 1972, p. 843). The major journal of the APS, *The Physical Review*, committed some 2,000 scientific papers to print in 1970—roughly one page for each of the society's 28,500 members (Interview with Edward Purcell, 1970).

Until recently, the presentation of papers at society meetings and regular publication in *The Physical Review* have been the only forms of participation in APS affairs through which young physicists could reasonably hope to gain recognition in their field. There have been, for example, very few society committees—through which appointed members can gain professional visibility—and membership on these few committees, as well as on the APS council, has been made up exclusively of "elder statesmen," whose well-established eminence in the field was prerequisite to their participation in society governance. Zuckerman and Merton (1971, p. 32) remind us that "scientific eminence and authority derive largely from past and not necessarily continuing accomplishments. In science then, as in other institutions, older men tend to have the power and authority." In the APS, as in the physics profession as a whole, a gerontocracy seems to prevail to an even greater extent than in many other academic associations and disciplines. Those physicists widely recognized to be among the most distinguished in their field are, to a notable degree, older scientists, many of whom achieved prominence in the period of dramatic scientific development immediately following World War II. One young physicist explained that in the period following the war

very young physicists got power and great importance early; a young man with the same talent today hasn't got the same chance or opportunity. These same men have held power for 25 years. They haven't developed a middle-management team of people in their 40s. There is a generation missing. In biology, there are young people who are rising in their 30s and 40s. In physics, there are only old men (Interview with Brian Schwartz, 1970).

The opportunity to join their ranks is enjoyed almost exclusively by younger physicists who succeed in winning the most coveted awards in their field, such as the Nobel Prize. Even for young physicists aspiring to a more modest position in the second or third ranks of the profession, work with distinguished senior scientists is essential to career advancement. It is this strong gerontocratic character of the physics profession that has been reflected in the pattern of participation in APS governance and that reduces the importance of the society as an organization through which new careers are launched.

As a result of the key role that nationally known physicists (including many APS officers and council members) have played since World War II as advisers to the government on federal science policy—serving, for example, on the influential President's Science Advisory Committee—the APS has had little need to develop organizational machinery for representing the interests of the scientific community to the government. Thus, although research in physics has been heavily supported by the federal government since the war, the APS has played a very minor role, as an organization, in promoting or guiding the distribution of this support. In fact, APS leadership has taken strict precautions to maintain an organizational posture of political detachment and neutrality, avoiding society activities or public statements that might be construed as lobbying or as attempts to exert political pressure. These efforts are officially justified in terms of the delicate and financially critical tax status of the APS as an educational organization. But it is also clear that the close ties of the physics profession with the federal government in the postwar period—and particularly its involvement in highly controversial defense research—have encouraged within the physics community a strong conviction of the value neutrality of science as an enterprise and a belief in the clear separability of scientific (or technical) issues and political ones. Under these conditions, the APS has assumed as one of its most critical functions in the discipline that of delineating and maintaining a sharp distinction between scientific and political concerns. Through a particularly strict and self-conscious delimitation of its own interests as being purely scientific, it has also avoided becoming embroiled in ethical questions regarding the consequences of physics research and averted the danger that its activities might offend or alienate government agencies providing vital support for work being done in physics.

THE FIRST SIGNS OF DISSIDENCE Like its counterparts in many other disciplines, the APS became embroiled in internal controversy in 1967 and 1968 over the issue of the Vietnam War. What distinguishes the emergence of the Vietnam issue in the APS, however, is that (1) it surfaced almost entirely through the persistence of one society member, who worked for over a year to bring the subject into open discussion within the organization; (2) the question of an organizational stand on Vietnam could be raised in only a very muted and indirect form within the context of the APS; and (3) organizational leadership was particularly reluctant (in comparison to the response in the APSA and the MLA, for example) to allow even open consideration of whether the Vietnam War was an appropriate issue to raise within the society.

The Schwartz Amendment In 1967, Charles Schwartz, a physicist of considerable stature from the University of California at Berkeley, wrote a letter to the editor of *Physics Today* (a journal published by the American Institute of Physics, an umbrella association of which the APS is the largest constituent) stating that he was concerned with the Vietnam War and thought it important that members of the APS begin to discuss the possibility of taking an organizational stand on this issue. The editor of *Physics Today* refused to publish his letter.

When Schwartz protested this omission to a number of APS officers, he was reminded that the constitutionally defined purposes of the society were the advancement and diffusion of knowledge and that the APS was formally prohibited from concerning itself with political questions. Schwartz determined, however, that an avenue was open for members to change the purposes of the society—the right of members to propose constitutional amendments.

Nearly a year after his initial letter was rejected, Schwartz presented a petition to the APS president (supported by the signatures of just over the required 1 percent of the society membership) proposing an amendment to the constitution. This amendment provided that "the members may express their opinion, will, or intent on any matter of concern to the Society by voting on one or several resolutions formally presented for their consideration..." ("Special Announcement," 1968, p. 9). Letters in support of, and in opposition to, the amendment were invited from the membership, with the special arrangement that a representative sample of views would be published in *Physics Today*. Despite the deliberately general wording of the Schwartz amendment, it was widely understood by society members to be an effort to promote discussion of the Vietnam War. The amendment was defeated in 1968 by a vote of 9, 214 to 3,553, the largest vote ever polled in the APS.

SCIENTISTS AND ENGINEERS FOR SOCIAL AND POLITICAL ACTION

At the early February meetings of the APS in 1969, a group of physicists, disappointed with the fate of the Schwartz amendment, met to form an organization, originally called Scientists for Social and Political Action, that was "concerned with the problems of today's world and seeking a radical redirection in the control of modern science and technology" (Scientists and Engineers for Social and Political Action, n.d.). Several hundred physicists attended the first meeting of this new organization. During the following year it was expanded to include engineers sympathetic to its objectives and subsequently came to be known as Scientists and Engineers for Social and Political Action (SESPA).

Dedicated to promoting a sense of social responsibility among American scientists, SESPA listed as its first concerns (1) the heavy government support of physics research related to the development of armaments and the threat posed to world peace by the products of this research; (2) the threat to the environment posed by the uncontrolled development of technology; and (3) the lack of organizational channels available to scientists and engineers through which to express their interests, their views on government policy, or their "moral responsibility to society at large" (Scientists and Engineers for Social and Political Action, n. d.). Protesting the proportionately small number of eminent physicists who, as government advisers, had been the sole representatives of the physics community to federal policy makers and whose views were generally taken to be the views of physicists as a whole, SESPA sought to provide an instrument through which a broader segment—and especially a *younger* segment—of the physics community could express its opinions to the government.

An important stimulus in the creation of SESPA was the precedent set by the emergence of caucuses in a number of other learned societies in the previous year, including the radical caucus in the Modern Language Association, whose founding session had been attended by, and had greatly impressed, Charles Schwartz. In its structure, however, SESPA was modeled after Students for a Democratic Society, with an emphasis on the formation of independent local groups of scientists whose activities were loosely coordinated by a national framework, but who were expected to take initiative in setting their own policies and programs. A common objective of these local groups was to combine political action with public education in an effort to confront environmental problems on the state and local level.

SESPA members were encouraged to "interact" with the American Physical Society and other professional associations wherever possible in a joint effort to challenge the relationship of these organizations to the military establishment and to turn their attention to their "neglected responsibilities to their members and to society" (Scientists and Engineers for Social and Political Action, n.d.). This interaction was never coordinated into a systematic effort to democratize the governance of the APS or to win office for SESPA members in the society; nor did SESPA, as such, organize or sponsor formal sessions at APS meetings. It was conceived, primarily, as a loosely organized alternative structure to the APS through which a wide range of dissidents might come together to discover or develop common objectives, but which imposed little uniformity or coordination upon their various perspectives or activities. Members were required only to commit themselves to the "SESPA Pledge": "I pledge that I will not participate in war research or weapons production. I further pledge to counsel my students and urge my colleagues to do the same."

The immediate issues that united SESPA members in 1969 were, most particularly, the Vietnam War, the events at the Democratic National Convention in Chicago the previous fall, and the heated controversy over the Antiballistic Missile System. These were the major concerns to which SESPA devoted its attention at the February meetings of the APS. And it was these issues that sustained a brief coalition within SESPA between a large number of scientists who referred to themselves as "liberal activists" and who made up the early leadership of the organization, and a group of radical activists, most of them graduate students and young research scientists.

One of the major objectives of SESPA members at the February 1969 meetings of the APS was to press the council to reconsider the question of moving the 1970 meetings of the society out of Chicago. Following the Democratic Convention, society leadership had received a large number of letters from members asking that the site of the 1970 convention be changed. The council had concluded, however, that such a gesture was inappropriate for a scholarly society and had voted to hold the meetings in Chicago as planned. In response to this action, 500 people packed the 1969 business meeting (later described as a "parliamentary nightmare") and passed a resolution urging the council to reconsider the question. (Since the business meeting of the APS has no formal power, actions taken there have the status only of recommendations for the council's consideration.) Ultimately, the council asked for an advisory referendum, and the matter was settled several months later when APS members voted not to abandon Chicago.

A founding member of SESPA, Brian Schwartz (professor of physics at MIT), also petitioned the council at its February 1969 meeting requesting the formation of a Division on the Problems of Physics and Society to be the equivalent of the society's six established divisions representing areas of specialization in physics. As a result, the Committee on the Problems of Physics and Society was created to organize discussion of public issues at APS meetings and to consider whether the creation of a new division was the most appropriate way to raise such issues within the society.

A second petition from Brian Schwartz requested that the APS schedule a session at its next meeting on the Technical Aspects of the Antiballistic Missile System. (The stress on the *technical* aspects of the system was a well-calculated attempt to avoid the charge that this subject was too political for inclusion in a scientific meeting.) A session on the ABM was immediately scheduled for the April meetings in Washington.

Another SESPA founder, Charles Schwartz (author of the Schwartz amendment), asked the council that a physicist under thirty years of age be elected to fellowship in the society so that he might then be nominated for councillor-at-large (a position open only to formally elected fellows). In response to the raising of this issue, the requirement of fellow status for elected society officers was dropped altogether by a constitutional amendment enacted in 1970. (These were the first instances of members of the APS directly petitioning the council in this manner, and the council meeting did not officially open until the petitioners had left the room. Two months later, however, the traditionally closed sessions of the council were opened to allow society members to observe the proceedings.)

The session devoted to the ABM at the society meetings in Washington two months later was something of a high point for SESPA in its relation with the APS. The ABM issue drew a large crowd to the meeting and generated lively debate. Despite the formal emphasis on the technical aspects of the ABM system, political issues were, of course, raised in the ensuing discussion, and SESPA members polled those attending the meeting to determine their views on this controversial issue.

In the course of that convention, some 30 members of SESPA also participated in a march on the Pentagon. Five of them were granted an interview with a Pentagon official, to whom they expressed their concern regarding the impact of military support on the direction of scientific research and their dismay at continuing projects to develop armaments.

By the time the APS met in Chicago in early 1970, interest in and concern about the issues of science and society had become both intense and widespread among those physicists attending the sessions. Descriptions of these meetings in *Physics Today* declared that "a new mood was evident at the Chicago meeting—one of activism and involvement in society" (Lubkin, 1970, p. 67) and that "concern and dissent over social issues were very much in the air" (Davis, 1970, p. 112). A special session on physics and society (officially sponsored by the APS) focused on urban and black problems and drew a large audience. SESPA organized a number of its own informal and unofficial discussions of political and social issues related to science, and groups of members distributed leaflets and petitions protesting (among other things) the Vietnam War.

However, few of the materials distributed at those meetings, even by SESPA members, identified SESPA as an organizational sponsor. Nor do the accounts of the meetings in *Physics Today* credit any particular organization with giving impetus or form to the dissent expressed there. For example, as part of a protest action planned by SESPA, some members carried signs into a meeting in which a physicist connected with military research was to speak. They were later identified only as "five men bearing placards" (Lubkin, 1970, p. 67). This anonymity reflects, in part, the SESPA policy of encouraging individual members to define and pursue their own objectives in relation to the APS, but it also points up the striking extent to which SESPA remained alien and peripheral to the mainstream of the physics discipline, even while many of the issues it raised were being granted a degree of legitimacy within the profession.

Events of the 1970 business meeting demonstrated the continued care of the APS to distinguish between those political issues that it would accept as appropriate for discussion within the physics community and those it would not. A motion to request the council to conduct a mail ballot of the membership on the Vietnam War was defeated, and a motion suggesting that the society lobby against the development of the supersonic transport (SST) was ruled out of order. However, a petition and a motion opposing military support of physics research were treated as relevant business and referred to the council for its consideration.

Two months later, the council accepted a new responsibility for aiding young physicists faced with a declining job market by establishing a Committee on Economic Concerns to examine the employment situation in physics and by issuing to members of the government and the press a statement protesting the current capriciousness of federal funding of science ("APS Statement," 1970).

SESPA Joins Science for the People

During 1969, the first year of SESPA's existence, its members had begun to develop local chapters, with the largest groups forming in Berkeley, Stanford, New York, and Boston. The

SESPA Newsletter was edited by Martin Perl, a Stanford physicist whose left-liberal orientation reflected the political posture of a large number of SESPA members during that period. The tone of the *Newsletter* was explicitly geared toward appealing to the left-liberal membership of the APS (guessed to be roughly a third of the total membership), in the hope of winning broad support for a reform movement both within the APS and outside of it (Interview with Martin Perl, 1973).

In 1970, however, editorship of the *SESPA Newsletter*, and the SESPA mailing list, were passed on to a Boston-based organization of scientists known as Science for the People, resulting in a merger of the two organizations and in a dramatic change of style for subsequent SESPA publications. Now edited by SESPA "collectives" in the Boston area, the *Newsletter* was expanded into a bimonthly journal—*Science for the People*—and took on a strong Marxist flavor. The first issue or two alienated most of the liberals who had been part of SESPA's early history. At this point, reformers committed to working within the society began to see SESPA as a potential threat to their own objectives. It was not only the socialist orientation of the group that now dominated SESPA but the willingness of its members to engage in militant and abrasive acts of protest within the APS that precluded the possibility of an active alliance with liberals in the society and that led to fears that SESPA would alienate all potential sources of support for an internal reform movement.

THE FORUM ON PHYSICS AND SOCIETY During 1970 and 1971, the APS Committee on the Problems of Physics and Society (created by the council in 1969) fulfilled its assigned task of organizing sessions at society meetings and discussing with the council the creation of a new Division on Physics and Society. Although the committee strongly recommended the establishment of such a division, the council hesitated to treat problems of physics and society as an area of specialization equivalent to the research specialties represented by existing divisions. They preferred a different kind of organ, one that all members of the society, regardless of their divisional affiliation, would feel free to join. They also wished to retain more authority over the activities of this body than they had over the operation of society divisions. The solution, officially approved in January of 1972, was the establishment of the Forum on Physics and Society, which was to provide an opportunity for all members of the society to discuss the interrelationship of physics, physicists, and society. The forum was explicitly prohibited, however, from making public statements in the name of the society (as are all divisions of the APS)—a clear indication that it was not conceived as an instrument through which to exert political pressure.

The officers of the forum in its first and second years included a number of the "liberal activists" who had participated in the founding of SESPA in 1969 and had since rejected the later, more radical posture of that organization. The chairman of the forum in 1973 was Martin Perl—the editor of the original *SESPA Newsletter*—who described himself as a "committed reformist," with little faith or interest in a major reorganization of society but a strong commitment to a reallocation of resources in science (Interview with Martin Perl, 1973).

One of the clearest mandates of the forum was that its executive committee would arrange sessions at APS meetings for the discussion of social and political issues of concern to scientists. And, as it happened, a session planned by a member of the executive committee for the April 1972 meetings of the society provided the first test of the relationship between the newly established forum and APS leadership. This session, dealing with the relationship of physicists to the Vietnam War, was to include four invited papers. When abstracts of these papers were submitted to the APS *Bulletin* for prior publication (a standard procedure for all papers to be presented at APS meetings), they were referred to the executive committee of the council for consideration, and their publication was vetoed. Since the inclusion of abstracts in the *Bulletin* is normally automatic, this omission was interpreted as an act of censorship and was strongly protested by members of the forum. The result was valuable publicity for the new organization and massive attendance at the April session on physicists and the war, where the four abstracts were distributed to members of the audience. "Without forethought on their part or ours," one forum member later wrote, "the Council had established us" (Callen, 1972, p. 9). By July of its first year in existence, the forum had acquired a membership of 1,000, making it comparable in size to several of the society's smaller divisions.

During the forum's first year, an attempt was also made within the APS (although not sponsored by the forum or supported by all its members) to amend the society's constitutional statement of goals in such a way as to "add further legitimacy to the efforts of the Forum by acknowledging that its activities are an integral part of the goals of the American Physical Society" (March 1972, p. 43). The amendment provided the following:

> The object of the Society shall be the advancement and diffusion of the knowledge of physics in order to increase man's understanding of nature and to contribute to the enhancement of the quality of life for all people. The Society shall assist its members in the pursuit of these humane goals and it shall shun those activities which are judged to contribute harmfully to the welfare of mankind ("The APS Amendment on Professional Responsibility," 1972).

A great deal of controversy over this amendment centered upon the ambiguity in its wording. It was not clear in what way, or through what form of sanction, objectionable activities were to be "shunned" by the society, or who was to judge—and on what basis—what would contribute harmfully to the welfare of mankind. Widespread concern over these fundamental questions contributed to the eventual defeat of the amendment.

Thus, while the forum was established as an instrument for introducing change in the APS, it was constrained in its objectives and activities by the necessity to function as a formal body within an organizational structure that remained essentially unchanged and within the framework of the traditional (constitutionally prescribed) purposes of that organization. Members of the forum executive committee were highly conscious of the restraints upon their activity and consistently sought ways to raise issues in the APS in a manner that would not alienate the council or the broader society membership. For example, sessions and symposia organized by the forum's program committee (on such topics as unemployment in physics, ecology, and government funding of physics research) were structured in such a way as to relate political issues closely to technical and professional ones. And while SESPA members were occasionally invited to participate in such sessions, their involvement was deliberately limited on the grounds that their militant and broadly political posture might offend forum audiences.

Most of the programs upon which the forum embarked reflected concerns that were, by this time, widespread among society members, and their activities, as well as their proposals for change were, on the whole, easily incorporated into the existing structure and purposes of the APS. For example, a forum Committee on Economic and Social Problems of the Profession undertook to study the employment problems of nontenured faculty members and research associates and to make recommendations to the council on the employment crisis, the need for manpower studies, and the need for guidelines for employers of physicists. One outcome of the work of this committee was that the council asked the forum to examine the operation of its placement service and its physics postdoctoral information pool and to suggest improvements in these services.

A Committee on Courses in Physics and Society was also established to compile syllabi, bibliographies, and source materials to be made available to teachers of courses on science and society.

A forum Study Group on Congressional Scientific Interns developed a proposal urging that the APS sponsor a Congressional Science Fellowship Program that would place two physicists each year in staff positions in the offices of members of Congress or of congressional committees, in order to provide Congress with much needed technical advice on scientific matters and to promote greater understanding among physicists of the science-policy process. One objective of this program was to enhance the prestige in the physics community of being well informed about the politics of science. The council's approval of this program in 1973, with an authorization of funds to support 2 one-year fellowships, was considered by forum members to be among their major accomplishments in the APS and demonstrated the legitimacy of the forum in the eyes of the physics establishment.

It is striking, however, that in its efforts to create new channels of communication between physicists and Congress, the forum found precedent in the Congressional Internship Program of the American Political Science Association—a program that the Caucus for a New Political Science had attempted (unsuccessfully) to abolish several years earlier. Where more radical caucuses such as CNPS were intent upon disengaging their associations from such ties with government, liberal reformers in the APS sought ways to gain a more representative voice for physicists (working through established political channels) in the framing of science policy. It was the conviction of forum members that research priorities must begin to be established within the scientific community and articulated through scientific organizations to government if scientists are to have any voice in the determination of such priorities. Only in this way might it be possible to divert federal support from research goals defined by the military to research of a more socially useful nature. One first step in this process was to find ways to educate scientists in the ways of Washington and the intricacies of the science-policy process.

THE IMPACT OF THE FORUM WITHIN THE APS

The mere establishment of a Forum on Physics and Society was, in itself, the most profound change to occur in the APS between 1968 and 1973. The existence of the forum reflected the legitimacy granted by the society to issues once defined as being entirely outside of its organizational purview. A new concern among physicists for their moral and social responsibility and for problems of unemployment in physics provided the impetus for both the creation of the forum and other developments in the APS that the forum helped to guide. Among these were the establishment of a number of APS committees dedicated to studying the state of the discipline and its learned society: an Economic Concerns Committee (which has undertaken a substantial manpower analysis program), a Committee on Women in Physics, a Committee on Minorities in Physics, and a Committee on the Future of the APS.

In 1973 the APS had clearly become more conscious of problems related to the welfare of its members and more concerned about the social responsibility of scientists and their professional organizations. The traditional governance structure of the society, however, remained essentially unchanged. The nominating committee had once again proposed one candidate for vice-president-elect (who would proceed automatically to the vice-presidency and then to the presidency of the APS), and forum members felt that attention must now be turned to introducing more democratic procedures into society governance. In fact, the forum executive committee had begun to discuss the possibility of running petition candidates for office. It remains to be seen whether the forum will become an effective instrument for bringing change to the structure of the APS.

7. The Academic Recession and the Future of American Learned Societies

The fall of 1970 marked the beginning of a shift in the preoccupation of both learned-society membership and leadership away from the ideological issues raised by the radical caucuses in 1967 and 1968 and toward the job crisis created in the disciplines by the academic recession. By 1970, the most extensive changes in association governance structure and policy that were to result from the radical/left-liberal challenge had already been formulated, if not implemented. New decision-making procedures and apparatus designed to widen participation and representation in the governance process had the not unanticipated effect of exerting more systematic control over the efforts of dissident groups, by placing new limits on what they could expect to accomplish through parliamentary maneuvering in the way of organizational reform. At the same time, the new left movement in the United States had lost momentum, so that the reduction of interest on the part of radical activists in politicizing American learned societies corresponded to a more general diminution of radical activism on the national scene.

1970 was also the first year in which the academic recession, and its impact on the job market for Ph.D.'s, became a central concern within disciplinary associations. The *Chronicle of Higher Education* (Scully, 1970, p. 1) announced in June:

College graduates, especially those completing their doctorates, are finding it harder to get jobs this spring than at any time in the previous decade.

New surveys indicate that while there is little actual unemployment among the doctoral recipients, they are struggling to find positions and in many cases are taking jobs they would have rejected in earlier years.

Association placement services reported a significant increase in the number of applicants for employment (including candidates who might in previous years have found jobs through other channels) and a decrease in the number of positions listed by employers.

SOURCES OF THE EMPLOYMENT CRISIS One of the first critical signs of an impending recession in higher education came in 1968, when the rate of increase of federal support for science research dropped abruptly from 10 to 0 percent, to rise again only slightly in 1972–73. The result of the increasing cost of the Vietnam War and of federal programs geared toward the alleviation of domestic urban problems and reflecting as well a diminution of public confidence in the value of unlimited scientific and technological development, this drastic reduction in the rate of growth of research support had an immediate impact on the budgets of universities with extensive federally subsidized science programs and on the operation of government-funded science research laboratories—both major sources of employment for Ph.D.'s in the physical sciences. Hardest hit were the sciences requiring the most expensive research equipment and facilities—most notably, physics.

At the same time, other economic trends had begun by the late 1960s to erode university budgets and to reduce the availability of both academic and nonacademic employment for Ph.D.'s in all fields. The enormous growth in higher education during the 1960s had greatly increased costs for American colleges and universities, while the simultaneous rise in the rate of general inflation eroded the dollars available to meet these costs. The expense of the Vietnam War, inflation, and a shift in national interest away from higher education to pressing urban and environmental problems combined to reduce federal appropriations for higher education, while inflation also produced cutbacks in state support for colleges and universities. Particularly on the state level, the student disruption provided a ready justification for reductions in public funding (Cheit, 1971).

One result of these converging financial pressures on higher education was a decrease, beginning in 1968, in the number of new faculty members hired each year, as many university departments adopted a policy of hiring only to fill vacancies. Consequently, the number of new faculty positions has risen very slowly since 1968, while the rate of production of Ph.D.'s has remained high. Wolfle and Kidd (1972) point out that one-half of the doctoral degrees awarded between 1861 and 1970 were awarded during the last nine years of that period and predict that the number awarded in 1971 to 1980 may be as large again as the figure for 1961 to 1970.

The implications of these combined trends for the availability of employment for Ph.D.'s in the 1970s (and perhaps the 1980s) are only too clear. And the situation is exacerbated by the probability that the undergraduate boom of the last decade and a half is now over. Projections indicate that the current leveling off of college enrollments will continue through the 1970s to be followed by a decline in the 1980s, and so smaller faculties will be required to teach undergraduates in the next 20 years (Watkins, 1973).

While the employment of Ph.D.'s in all academic fields has been affected by university budget cutting and by the leveling off of enrollments, these factors have played a more important part in the employment crisis in the humanities and the social sciences than they have in the natural sciences. The physical sciences, in particular, have been heavily dependent upon government support in the postwar period, and so the most important single influence on the job shortage in fields such as physics has been cutbacks in federal allocations for research and development. Nearly 40 percent of the Ph.D.'s in physics were employed outside of colleges and universities in 1967–68 (Strassenburg, 1970), while over 50 percent were engaged primarily in research and development activities (Koch, 1970, p. 26) for which the government has been the major source of support. The negative effects of the recession on industrial funding for science have also contributed to the employment crisis in physics, although their greatest impact has been on fields such as chemistry and engineering, in which employment in industry has far exceeded both government and academic employment (ibid.).

In the humanities, by contrast, roughly 90 percent of all doctoral recipients have been employed as teachers in universities and colleges. [For example, 92 percent of the doctorates in English held academic teaching posts in 1968 ("Doctoral Surveys," 1973).] As a result, employment for Ph.D.'s in fields such as English and the modern languages has been most directly affected by reductions in enrollment and departmental budget cutting. In addition, these two fields have felt the impact of the recent trend toward the "liberalization" of undergraduate curricula, leading to the widespread elimination of English and foreign language requirements for undergraduates and to a reduced demand for faculty to teach introductory courses ("Freshman English Requirements," 1971; "FL Requirements and Enrollments," 1971).

In further contrast to the sciences, the humanities, which have enjoyed little federal support for research in the postwar years, have been little affected by either cutbacks in federal research funds or the industrial recession.

The percentage of social science Ph.D.'s employed in academic teaching falls somewhere between that for natural scientists and that for Ph.D.'s in the humanities. Roughly three-quarters of political scientists, anthropologists, and sociologists are employed by colleges and universities, a large proportion of these in a teaching capacity. Thus, employment in the social sciences has been more seriously influenced by the squeeze on university funds than by reductions in federal or industrial funding, although the latter trends have played a secondary part in the job shortage for social scientists.

THE NATURE OF THE JOB CRISIS AND ITS IMPACT ON LEARNED SOCIETIES

While surveys of the employment situation for Ph.D.'s revealed little actual unemployment between 1968 and 1972, there are clear indications that jobs had become much harder to find and that more Ph.D.'s had begun to accept positions that they would not have found acceptable a few years earlier, that failed to meet their job expectations, and, in some cases, that did not utilize the professional competence they had acquired through graduate training. The National Research Council reported, for example, that among recipients of the Ph.D. in science and engineering, 71.5 percent of the 1968 graduates found employment that generally utilized their professional expertise, and 68.7 percent of the 1969 graduates found such employment. At the same time, the number of graduates in temporary postdoctoral positions rose from 11 to 17.7 percent in those two years (Scully, 1970).

The pattern of employment for Ph.D.'s in English also reflected a downward trend in the types of institutions in which graduates found positions. A survey conducted by the Modern

Language Association in 1972 revealed that 47.7 percent of 1971–72 doctorates had obtained posts in universities, 35.7 percent in four-year colleges, and 5.1 percent in two-year colleges, in contrast to figures provided by a comparable study in 1968, which indicated that of recent recipients of the Ph.D., 62.6 percent had obtained positions in universities, 29.4 percent in four-year colleges, and only 0.4 percent in two-year colleges ("Doctoral Surveys," 1973).

Less well documented by survey data has been the impact of the Ph.D. surplus on untenured junior faculty, who have felt their job security to be severely threatened by departmental budgetary problems, by a general tightening up of tenure policies, and by the ease with which they can be replaced from among the burgeoning ranks of job-seeking Ph.D.'s.

Cutbacks in federal and industrial research and development programs also stranded large numbers of experienced scientists, who have been forced to compete on the job market with new graduates. A survey conducted by the American Physical Society in 1970 and 1971 suggested that "the main burden of the present employment crisis is being borne by the more experienced physicist." In 1970, 1,700 experienced Ph.D.'s joined 1,500 new Ph.D.'s in the search for jobs, and of the total, 30 percent failed to find employment (Lubkin, 1971).

Consequently, demands upon American disciplinary associations to assist their members in the face of the job crisis came both from new Ph.D.'s searching for first employment and from young professors and nonacademically employed Ph.D.'s who had lost jobs or who were fearful of impending unemployment. Many members of these groups made the initial assumption that, if mobilized on their behalf, learned societies could assist them substantially by locating new sources of employment, by prescribing and enforcing guidelines for employers that would protect their rights as employees, and by taking steps to curtail the continuing overproduction of Ph.D.'s by graduate departments. Some even suggested (as did members of the job caucus in the Modern Language Association) that their associations assume responsibility for financially compensating unemployed members of the disciplinary professions.

Despite the investment of available association resources in improving job exchange services, in elaborate job market and manpower studies, in formulating recommendations for reducing graduate enrollments, and in framing guidelines for employers, however, disciplinary associations were generally able to do little more than reaffirm the existence of a serious job shortage and to play an important part in publicizing it. What immediately became evident was the lack of resources or machinery available for organizational action that would significantly alleviate the job crisis. Given the general nature of the recession and the wide impact of inflation on the economy of the nation as a whole, few new reservoirs of employment opportunity could be readily opened up to Ph.D.'s through association research or through attempts to redefine and broaden the jurisdiction of the various disciplines. Nor could disciplinary associations wield commanding influence over departmental policies and practices affecting recruitment of graduate students, recruitment of faculty, or the granting of tenure. These practices are too closely tied to intrauniversity policy and to critical budgetary matters to be strongly responsive to the exhortations of national disciplinary organizations. In some cases, wider listing of available academic posts resulted from association urging that competition for such jobs be opened up nationally, but there is little evidence that this trend reflected any major change in the "old boy" system through which most prestigious university departments have traditionally recruited.

At the same time, many learned societies were themselves experiencing severe budgetary problems as a result of inflation and of the increased cost of new governance procedures and apparatus (including more elaborate committee structures) that had grown out of the events of the late 1960s. Financial distress was reported by officers of the American Political Science Association and of the Modern Language Association in 1970, and, in both cases, the budgetary crisis led to immediate reductions in allocations for committee work—including support for committees on women, blacks, and, in the MLA, for the new Advisory Committee on the Job Market. The financial pinch on these learned societies placed an important limit on the resources that could be appropriated for the study or alleviation of minority-group problems, or the wider job shortage.[1]

---

[1] Budgetary problems seemed to be less severe in the American Physical Society by 1970, where serious deficits had been encountered a year or two earlier. The immediate adoption of new and less costly printing procedures had reduced expenses for the society's mammoth publication program, releasing funds for use to support new society projects (Walsh, 1973).

Impact of the Recession on Radical Activities

Given the general diminution of radical activism in the United States by 1970, it is difficult to assess the additional impact of the academic recession on further expressions of radical dissent either within universities or within national organizations representing the disciplines. It is striking, however, that among the radical intellectuals and left-liberals who continued to work actively toward reform within American learned societies after 1970, there remained few graduate students or young, untenured faculty members. Leadership of such bodies as the Caucus for a New Political Science and the Forum in the American Physical Society came to be composed almost exclusively of well-established professors, one of whom asked in perplexity at a 1972 meeting of CNPS, "Where are all the dangerous young men?" One plausible answer is that young radicals and left-liberals who might have sought colleagueship through some form of participation in these reform groups began to feel constrained by job insecurity from identifying themselves ideologically. Both Wolfe (1970) and Landers and Cicarelli (1970) have pointed to the pressure on untenured faculty in an unfavorable job market to appear politically "safe" to present and prospective employers—a pressure intensified by widespread rumors of "political" firings and of other repressive actions against radicals. At one informal meeting of the Radical Caucus in English and the Modern Languages at the annual MLA convention in 1972, a number of young faculty members urged discussion of the job problems facing radical teachers, asserting that only if the caucus devoted itself seriously to employment issues could it hope to have any base of support among young academics. There were also frequent references (in a more private vein) to colleagues who did not attend the caucus meetings because they were looking for jobs and felt they could not risk being identified with radical activity.

If the recession can indeed be assumed to have discouraged some younger members of the disciplines from participation in dissident activity within their learned societies, it does not seem to have had the same effect upon more anonymous forms of support for caucus campaigns and programs. For example, as indicated in the previous case studies, the Caucus for a New Political Science continued into the 1970s to win a sizable vote for its annual candidate for president of the American Political Science Association (based no doubt on his or her appeal to a wide range of liberals within the political science profession), and the physics forum had also attained an impressive membership by 1972. By having made the employment crisis one of its own central concerns, in fact, the forum may have gained general membership support from young physicists with a primary interest in the job situation.

THE TREND TOWARD FACULTY UNIONISM Ultimately, the most serious implications of the academic recession for the future character and focus of American disciplinary associations seem to lie in the academic union movement, which gained considerable momentum in the early 1970s as a result of deteriorating conditions of work for academic faculties. Ladd and Lipset (1973) pointed to the rapid growth of unionization and collective bargaining in higher education, citing an estimate from Aussieker and Garbarino (1973) that roughly one-sixth of the academic faculty in the United States was represented by unions in 1973 (by the American Federation of Teachers, the National Education Association, and the American Association of University Professors) and that the number was rising steadily.

Ladd and Lipset link the rise of academic unionism with the new conditions of fiscal austerity in higher education in the 1970s—to heightened job insecurity for young faculty, lags in salary increases, and heavier teaching loads—but attribute this trend as well to the heightened bureaucratization of the university that accompanied the rapid growth of the 1960s, to the critical legislative actions in the sixties that established bargaining rights for public employees in higher education, and, importantly, to "the sudden growth of militant egalitarian movements among the intellectually oriented strata—including college students—related to the Civil Rights movement, and particularly to the opposition to the Vietnam War" (Ladd & Lipset, 1973, p. 4). Indeed, the union movement has become one locus of action for ex-members of the New University Conference and for both present and one-time participants in radical caucus activity in learned societies (including continuing members of the Radical Caucus in English and the Modern Languages—see Chapter 5), despite the fact (also stressed by Ladd and Lipset) that faculty unionization represents a conservative trend in higher education with respect to the bid for student power.[2]

As the union movement expands, it provides an increasingly important alternative to learned societies as a major form of faculty organization. Competing for membership from the same general population, unions represent egalitarian norms that are almost diametrically opposed to the professional and scholarly norms and values of disciplinary associations. The latter organizations have promoted the prestige of the disciplines, stressing above all the necessity for work autonomy for scholars and scientists engaged in advancing knowledge and relying on national disciplinary prestige to assure their members high salaries and other favorable conditions of employment within academic institutions. At the same time, they have promoted status differentiation within the disciplines, allocating status rewards among their members on the basis of individual scholarly accomplishment and excellence. Faculty unions, on the other hand, deemphasize both disciplinary distinctions and status distinctions among their members, relying more heavily upon the strength of collective action than upon disciplinary or individual prestige to gain benefits within the university. In the process, claims to individual and disciplinary autonomy are also deemphasized in favor of more tangible collective rewards related to salary, work loads, and job security.

Since learned societies have traditionally taken for granted the favorable bargaining position of their members as individual scholars and scientists, they have devoted little attention to strengthening this position except insofar as they have sought to strengthen the relative prestige of their disciplines nationally. Thus, in a period of academic retrenchment, when the general bargaining position of college and university faculties is on the decline and conditions of academic employment are deteriorating, unions have begun to seem a more appropriate form of organization for a large segment of the nation's faculty,

---

[2] Faculty unions have been accused of providing a means of collective defense against the demands of students, at the same time that they have acted as bargaining agents in relation to employers, by excluding students from negotiations concerning conditions of faculty employment that directly affect their interests and by undermining the role that students had begun to gain in campus decision making in the 1960s (Semas, 1973).

particularly for those academics whose personal bargaining power is most limited—who hold less preferred positions in the academic system or whose employment is most precarious.

For example, as junior, nontenured faculty find their bargaining position vis-à-vis academic employers seriously weakened by an unfavorable job market, they are faced with diminishing chances of ever achieving high status positions in academia. Under these conditions, they are likely to attain greater employment benefits from participation in collective bargaining activities than from a strong identification with national scholarly associations. Not only do learned societies lack the machinery to deal with the bread-and-butter issues that now preoccupy their younger members, but for most young Ph.D.'s in the disciplines, participation in the scholarly activities of these associations no longer holds out the promise of career rewards that it did during the postwar period of academic expansion and mobility.

In addition, those discipline members whose status in the academic system has been relatively low (professors in low-prestige four-year colleges and in junior colleges and those on the periphery of core university faculties) have more to gain from union organization—which can significantly enhance their bargaining position in academic institutions (Garbarino, 1972)—than from membership in national disciplinary associations. It is these academicians, who have been most marginal to the operation of learned societies, who have wielded the least influence in them and have benefited the least in terms of status rewards from their membership.

It is senior faculty members at high-prestige institutions —the group occupying the most preferred position in academia—whose employment status is least threatened by the academic recession and who stand to gain the least from the current proliferation of collective bargaining units on campus. While some members of this high achievement group are finding it increasingly necessary to participate in union negotiations to assure the representation of their interests there, they have, for the most part, only "shored up some of their benefits from possible attack, but otherwise have gained the least from bargaining" (ibid.). This group has also consistently dominated the prestige and leadership structure in learned societies and continues to reap the most significant rewards from a strong commitment to the national disciplinary networks that these associations represent.

Given the possibility that under present employment conditions only those faculty members at the top of the academic hierarchy will sustain a primary identification with national disciplinary organizations, while the majority of academics will have increasing incentive to identify more strongly with, and to participate more actively in, the local units of collective bargaining agencies, it seems reasonable to predict that the size and character of learned-society memberships will undergo major change in the next decade. In fact, as white-collar unionism expands to encompass more Ph.D.'s employed by industry and government, they, too, may find learned societies less relevant professional organizations and thus contribute to the reversal of the postwar patterns of membership expansion and diversification and to making learned societies once again the more exclusive domain of eminent scholars and scientists from the nation's elite colleges and universities.

To the extent that such a contraction in membership will occur, it will have crucial implications, as well, for the range of activities that national disciplinary associations can be expected to engage in. A reduction in membership means, of course, a reduction in income from dues and suggests a future necessity to cut back on both the size of association staffs and the kinds of services that these organizations will provide their members—a reversal, as well, of the trend of the 1950s and 1960s toward the expansion of facilities and of instrumental activities. At the same time, there will be less demand upon these organizations for such membership benefits as group insurance and travel programs as these kinds of benefits are incorporated into the employment contracts negotiated by faculty unions. And, more importantly, pressures on learned societies to deal with broader issues related to membership employment—including equal employment opportunity for groups previously underrepresented in academia—will decrease as the domain of the union movement expands. To be effective in their quest for equal academic employment, women and minority groups will find it increasingly necessary to focus their attention upon faculty unions as agencies through which to enhance their position.

It also seems less likely in the 1970s than it did in the boom years of the 1960s that disciplinary associations will find it possible to develop or maintain staff and machinery with the specific function of monitoring federal government activity or lobbying, or that they will move further in the direction of developing expensive certification and accreditation programs such as those provided by fully professionalized associations in the United States.

A contraction of learned-society membership and activities also implies a reduced need for the elaborate governance apparatus—including the expanded committee structure—that emerged in response to the organizational growth of the 1950s and 1960s and to the dissident activity of the last five years.

These are grounds for speculating, then, that learned societies will once again begin to focus more exclusively on activities and programs related to the advancement and diffusion of knowledge—most importantly, on the publication of journals and the arrangement of annual scholarly meetings. But here, too, inflation and the squeeze on university funds can be expected to have an impact. The now extensive publication programs of many of these associations will suffer from a reduced base of support and may have to be pruned (for example, by the elimination of some specialized journals) unless they can somehow be made financially independent of income from membership dues. And the diminishing availability of university travel funds portends much smaller attendance at national meetings. It is possible, in fact, that the reduction in available funds for travel will lend impetus to the expansion of regional affiliates of the national disciplinary associations, which can provide their members with easier access to scholarly meetings and to cosmopolitan colleagueship, and with the opportunity for exchanging new knowledge.

Regional associations are also likely to become more important loci for the exchange of jobs, although there are still indications at present that the job exchange services provided by national learned societies will continue to be in great demand in an unfavorable job market situation. These services may draw considerable numbers of job-seeking Ph.D.'s into short-term membership in national disciplinary organizations as long as they are found to be fruitful sources of employment.

CONCLUSION Learned societies have been closely linked in American higher education with the development of an academic value and prestige system that gives first priority to the production of knowledge and to the training of scholars and scientists to engage in research. During the peak years of academic growth—the decades following World War II—these associations became central professional organizations for a rising number of Ph.D.'s in the disciplines for whom career advancement in their fields was closely tied to the research-oriented reward system in which learned societies played a critical role. And, at the same time, national disciplinary associations defined the scholastic standards and criteria according to which new and upwardly mobile college and university departments sought to enhance their standing in the academic hierarchy. Through the 1960s, the combined conditions of academic prosperity and an unwavering national commitment to research and graduate training placed learned societies in a key position of influence in the expanding higher education system—a position that prompted radical and left-liberal reformers, as well as women and minority groups, to view these societies as strategic organizations through which to initiate change in academia.

The erosion of both of these conditions in the 1970s suggests the likelihood, however, that the centrality of disciplinary associations within the academic enterprise will diminish in the next decades. Not only may the union movement hold out more substantial rewards for large numbers of faculty members, but the research-oriented prestige system that the learned societies have buttressed and promoted is now under assault from outside as well as within academia. As suggested above, the shift in national priorities away from the support of higher education—and particularly of academic research—reflects a growing national concern for pressing social and environmental problems for which basic research is no longer thought to hold the key. And as the prestige of academic research diminishes in the public eye, there is increasing pressure from important external constituencies of the university—including state legislatures and the federal government—to reduce expensive graduate and research programs in favor of the development of programs with a more immediate service function: undergraduate education, continuing education, vocational training, and community service. This thrust toward a reordering of academic priorities now receives support within academia from college and university administrators, who must concern themselves with the financial viability of their institutions in a period of recession, as well as from students and left-oriented faculty members who have urged a stronger focus on the teaching of undergraduates and the involvement of the university in social reform.

This is not to suggest that the academic reward structure, which stresses scholarly and scientific achievement, will be completely overwhelmed by the emergence of a new value orientation in higher education. Rather, nationally prestigious graduate training and research programs may well become a smaller part of the operation of even major American universities; the national reputation of individual scholars and scientists and of academic departments will become a less exclusive source of prestige for the institutions that house them; fewer undergraduate schools will aspire to national distinction by emulating the model of the research-oriented graduate university; and finally, fewer academics will seek professional advancement through the research-and-publication route as alternative career patterns and rewards become available to them.

Thus, at the same time that changing conditions of academic employment promote the expansion of union organization in higher education, a realignment of academic priorities also undermines the hegemony of the research orientation as the core value of American learned societies. As the production of knowledge becomes the major professional commitment of a smaller group within the disciplines, disciplinary associations will, correspondingly, wield influence within a narrower sphere of academic life. Nevertheless, there seems little reason to doubt that specialized, cosmopolitan scholarship will remain a vital—albeit less preeminent—force in American higher education or that learned societies will continue to play a crucial role in fostering and sustaining this commitment.

References

"Actions of the 1968 Business Meeting," *PMLA*, vol. 84, no. 5, pp. 1231–1233, September 1969.

American Anthropologist, vol. 43, no. 2, pt. 1, April–June 1941; vol. 53, no. 3, July–September 1951.

American Historical Association: *Annual Report*, 1940, 1950, 1960.

American Political Science Review, vol. 35, no. 1, February 1941; vol. 45, no. 4, December 1951.

American Sociological Review, vol. 5, no. 4, August 1940; vol. 15, no. 6, December 1950; vol. 25, no. 6, December 1960.

"The APS Amendment on Professional Responsibility," *Physics Today*, vol. 25, no. 11, pp. 42–49, November 1972.

"APS Statement," *Bulletin of the American Physical Society*, ser. 2, vol. 15, no. 5, pp. 870–871, May 1970.

Aussieker, Bill, and Joseph W. Garbarino: "Measuring Faculty Unionism: Quantity and Quality," article published by the Institute of Business and Economic Research, Berkeley, Calif., May 1973.

"Ballot on Resolutions," *MLA Newsletter*, vol. 2, no. 2, p. 7, March 1970.

Barton, H. A.: "The Story of the American Institute of Physics," *Physics Today*, vol. 9, no. 1, pp. 56–66, January 1956.

Baskin, Darryl: "American Pluralism: Theory, Practice, and Ideology," *Journal of Politics*, vol. 32, no. 1, pp. 71–95, February 1970.

Bay, Christian: "For an American *Political* Science Association," *P.S.*, vol. 1, no. 3, pp. 36–38, Summer 1968.

Bayer, Ronald, et al.: "Communications," *P.S.*, vol. 1, no. 1, pp. 38–40, Winter 1968.

Birnbaum, Norman: "Reviews," *Change*, vol. 2, no. 4, pp. 60–67, July–August 1970.

Bloland, Harland G.: "National Associations and the Shaping of Federal Higher Education Policy," *Sociology of Education,* vol. 41, no. 2, pp. 156–177, Spring 1968.

Callen, Earl: "Social Action in the American Physical Society," a paper presented at the meetings of the American Association for the Advancement of Science, Washington, D. C., Dec. 28, 1972.

Cantarow, Ellen: "The Radicalizing of a Teacher of Literature," *Change,* vol. 4, no. 4, pp. 50–61, May 1972.

The Caucus for a New Political Science: *Newsletter,* vol. 2, no. 1, pp. 4–5, October 1968.

Cheit, Earl F.: *The New Depression in Higher Education: A Study of Financial Conditions at 41 Colleges and Universities,* McGraw-Hill Book Company, New York, 1971.

College English, vol. 34, no. 2, pp. 169–317, November 1972.

Commission on the Status of Women in the Profession: "Report to the Business Meeting, December 1970," *MLA Newsletter,* vol. 3, no. 1, pp. 1–4, February 1971.

Committee on the Status of Blacks in the Profession: Statement distributed at the annual meeting of the APSA, Los Angeles, September 1970.

Davis, Harold L.: "Consensus at Chicago," *Physics Today,* vol. 23, no. 3, p. 112, March 1970.

Dixon, Marlene: "Academic Roles and Functions," *The Insurgent Sociologist,* vol. 2, no. 2, pp. 8–17, Spring 1972.

"Doctoral Surveys," *MLA Newsletter,* vol. 5, no. 1, p. 4, February 1973.

Fisher, John Hurt: "The Modern Language Association of America, 1883–1968," *ACLS Newsletter,* vol. 20, no. 2, pp. 19–25, March 1969.

"FL Requirements and Enrollments," *MLA Newsletter,* vol. 3, no. 5, p. 7, November 1971.

"Freshman English Requirements," *MLA Newsletter,* vol. 3, no. 5, p. 2, November 1971.

Garbarino, Joseph W.: "Faculty Unionism: From Theory to Practice," *Industrial Relations,* vol. 2, no. 1, pp. 1–17, February 1972.

Gilb, Corinne Lathrop: *Hidden Hierarchies,* Harper & Row, Publishers, Incorporated, New York, 1966.

Harold, Brent: "On Our Situation at Present," *Radical Caucus in English and the Modern Languages: Newsletter #8,* pp. 2–3, March 1973.

Herzberg, Donald, for the Ad Hoc Committee for a Representative Slate: Letter to the APSA Membership, n.d. (Mimeographed.)

"Historical Perspectives Behind the Assembly's 85 Theses," *The Chronicle of Higher Education*, p. 10, Jan. 18, 1971.

Homans, George C.: "Report of the President," *American Sociological Review*, vol. 29, no. 6, p. 895, December 1964.

Howe, Florence: "An Open Letter from the MLA President," *MLA Newsletter*, vol. 5, no. 2, p. 11, March 1973.

Hux, Samuel: "The English Journals and the Specialty Syndrome," *Change*, vol. 5, no. 4, pp. 54–56, May 1973.

Income Tax Regulations as of July 25, 1967, "Final" and "Proposed" Under Internal Revenue Code, vol. 1, no. 1.01–1.855(f), Commerce Clearing House, Chicago, 1967.

Jencks, Christopher, and David Riesman: *The Academic Revolution*, Doubleday & Company, Inc., Garden City, N.Y., 1968.

Kampf, Louis: "The Trouble with Literature...," *Change*, vol. 2, no. 3, pp. 27–34, May–June 1970.

Kampf, Louis, and Florence Howe: "Expression of Opinion on the Delegate Assembly," *MLA Newsletter*, vol. 3, no. 1, p. 5, February 1971.

Kettler, David: Letter to Vernon Van Dyke, February 26, 1969*a*.

Kettler, David: Letter to the Editor, *P.S.*, vol. 2, no. 1, p. 47, Winter 1969*b*.

Kettler, David: Letter to the Editor, *The Chronicle of Higher Education*, p. 3, November 23, 1970*a*.

Kettler, David: "The Vocation of Radical Intellectuals," *Politics and Society*, vol. 1, no. 1, pp. 23–49, November 1970*b*.

Klotsburger, Katherine M.: Letter to the Editor, *P.S.*, vol. 4, no. 3, pp. 493–494, Summer 1971.

Koch, H. William: "On Physics and Employment of Physicists in 1970," *Physics Today*, vol. 24, no. 6, pp. 23–27, June 1971.

Ladd, Everett Carll, Jr., and Seymour Martin Lipset: *Professors, Unions, and American Higher Education*, Carnegie Commission on Higher Education, Berkeley, Calif., 1973.

Landers, Clifford E., and James S. Cicarelli: "Academic Recession," *The New Republic*, vol. 162, no. 19, pp. 14–16, May 9, 1970.

Lauter, Paul: "For Future Reference," in *The Radical Teacher*, published by the New University Conference, Chicago, pp. 1 and 17, 1969.

Lowi, Theodore J.: "Who *Should* Govern," *P.S.*, vol. 2, no. 3, pp. 276–277, Summer 1969.

Lubkin, Gloria B.: "Chicago Meeting Involved with Society," *Physics Today*, vol. 23, no. 3, pp. 67–69, March 1970.

Lubkin, Gloria B.: "Job Shortage Hits Older Physicists Hardest," *Physics Today,* vol. 24, no. 5, pp. 61–63, May 1971.

March, Robert H.: Letter to the Editor, *Physics Today,* vol. 25, no. 11, pp. 42–43, November 1972.

New University Conference: "Educational Research: Educational Change?" Statement distributed at meetings of the American Educational Research Association, pp. 1–3, n.d.

"1971 APS Finances," *Bulletin of the American Physical Society,* ser. 2, vol. 17, no. 9, pp. 842–843, September 1972.

"Observations by Louis Kampf," *MLA Newsletter,* vol. 1, no. 3, pp. 3–4, October 1969.

Ohmann, Richard: "The MLA and the Politics of Inadvertence," *PMLA,* vol. 83, no. 4, pt. 1, pp. 988–990, September 1968*a.*

Ohmann, Richard: *Politics and Professional Organizations: A Radical View,* distributed by the Modern Language Caucus of the New University Conference, 1968*b.*

Ohmann, Richard: "An Informal and Perhaps Unreliable Account of the Modern Language Association of America," *The Antioch Review,* vol. 29, no. 3, pp. 329–347, Fall 1969.

Ohmann, Richard: "Teaching and Studying Literature at the End of Ideology," pp. 130–159, in Louis Kampf and Paul Lauter (eds.), *The Politics of Literature,* Pantheon Books, a division of Random House, Inc., New York, 1970.

Orlans, Harold: *Contracting for Knowledge,* Jossey-Bass Publishers, Inc., San Francisco, 1973.

Parsons, Talcott: 'The Editor's Column," *The American Sociologist,* vol. 1, no. 3, pp. 124–126, May 1966.

Publications of the Modern Language Association, vol. 75, no. 4, part 2, September 1960; vol. 85, no. 3, May 1970*a;* vol. 85, no. 4, September 1970*b;* vol. 86, September 1971.

"Report of the Executive Committee," *American Political Science Review,* vol. 61, no. 2, pp. 565–568, June 1967.

"Report of the Executive Director, 1968–69," *P.S.,* vol. 2, special supplement, pp. 479–537, Summer 1969.

"Report of the Executive Secretary," *PMLA,* vol. 84, no. 4, pp. 677–680, June 1969.

"Report of the Treasurer for the Fiscal Year July 1, 1968–June 30, 1969," *P.S.,* vol. 2, special supplement, pp. 558–563, Summer 1969.

"Report of the Treasurer, July 1, 1969–June 30, 1970," *P.S.,* vol. 3, special issue, pp. 592–599, Summer 1970.

"Report of the Trustees and of the Treasurer," *PMLA*, vol. 83, no. 3, pp. 540–545, June 1968.

"Reports on the MLA," *Radical Caucus in English and the Modern Languages: Newsletter #6*, p. 1, Jan. 4, 1973.

Schorske, Carl E.: "Professional Ethos and Public Crisis: A Historian's Reflections," *PMLA*, vol. 83, no. 4, pt. 1, pp. 979–984, September 1968.

Scientific and Technical Societies of the United States and Canada, 7th ed., publication 900, compiled by John H. Gribbin and others, National Academy of Sciences-National Research Council, Washington, D.C., 1961.

Scientists and Engineers for Social and Political Action: leaflet, n.d.

Scully, Malcolm G.: "Modern Language, History Associations Weigh Questions of Political Involvement," *The Chronicle of Higher Education*, vol. 3, no. 9, p. 5, Jan. 13, 1969.

Scully, Malcolm G.: "Graduates Find It Takes 'Hard Digging' to Get Jobs; Many Ph.D.'s Accept Temporary University Posts," *The Chronicle of Higher Education*, vol. 4, no. 35, pp. 1 and 8, June 8, 1970.

"Secretary's Elucidation," *MLA Newsletter*, vol. 1, no. 2, p. 2, May 1969.

Semas, Philip W.: "Students Consider Own Bargaining Role as Faculty Units Dominate Key Issues," *The Chronicle of Higher Education*, vol. 7, no. 30, p. 4, Apr. 30, 1973.

Shor, Ira: "Notes on Marxism and Method," *College English*, vol. 34, no. 2, pp. 173–177, November 1972.

Smith, Henry Nash: "Statement by Henry Nash Smith, 1969 MLA President," *PMLA*, vol. 84, no. 2, p. 344, March 1969.

Somit, Albert, and Joseph Tanenhaus: *The Development of American Political Science: From Burgess to Behavioralism*, Allyn and Bacon, Inc., Boston, 1967.

"Special Announcement," *Bulletin of the American Physical Society*, ser. 2, vol. 13, no. 1, p. 9, Jan. 29, 1968.

Strassenburg, Arnold A.: "Supply and Demand for Physicists," *Physics Today*, pp. 23–28, April 1970.

Surkin, Marvin, and Alan Wolfe: "The Political Dimension of American Political Science," *Acta Politica*, vol. 5, no. 1, pp. 43–61, October 1969.

Surkin, Marvin, and Alan Wolfe (eds.): *An End to Political Science: The Caucus Papers*, Basic Books, Inc., Publishers, New York, 1970.

Walsh, John: "American Physical Society," *Science*, vol. 180, no. 4086, pp. 576–577, May 11, 1973.

Ward, Paul L.: "Minutes of the Council Meeting, April 4, 1970," *AHA Newsletter*, vol. 8, no. 5, pp. 1–8, June 1970.

Wasson, Richard: "New Marxist Criticism: Introduction," *College English*, vol. 34, no. 2, pp. 169–172, November 1972.

Watkins, Beverly T.: "Future College Enrollments Now Seen Falling Far Short of Previous Projections," *The Chronicle of Higher Education*, vol. 8, no. 2, pp. 1 and 6, Oct. 1, 1973.

"Why an MLA Newsletter?" *MLA Newsletter*, vol. 1, no. 1, p. 2, March 1969.

Wolfe, Alan: "Practicing the Pluralism We Preach: Internal Processes in the American Political Science Association," *The Antioch Review*, vol. 29, no. 3, pp. 353–373, Fall 1969.

Wolfe, Alan: "The Ph.D. Glut: Hard Times on Campus," *The Nation*, vol. 210, no. 20, pp. 623–627, May 25, 1970.

Wolfe, Alan: "Unthinking about the Thinkable: Reflections on the Failure of the Caucus for a New Political Science," *Politics and Society*, vol. 1, no. 3, pp. 393–406, May 1971.

Wolfle, Dael, and Charles V. Kidd: "The Future Market for Ph.D.'s," *AAUP Bulletin*, vol. 58, no. 1, pp. 5–16, Spring 1972.

Zuckerman, Harriet: "Stratification in American Science," *Sociological Inquiry*, vol. 40, no. 2, pp. 235–257, Spring 1970.

Zuckerman, Harriet, and Robert Merton: "Sociology of Refereeing," *Physics Today*, vol. 24, no. 7, pp. 28–33, July 1971.

Bibliography

Baskin, Darryl: "American Pluralism: Theory, Practice, and Ideology," *Journal of Politics,* vol. 32, no. 1, pp. 71–95, February 1970.

Bay, Christian: "For an American *Political* Science Association," *P.S.,* vol. 1, no. 3, pp. 36–38, Summer 1968.

Bittner, Egon: "Radicalism and the Organization of Radical Movements," *American Sociological Review,* vol. 28, no. 6, pp. 928–940, December 1963.

Bloland, Harland G.: "National Associations and the Shaping of Federal Higher Education Policy," *Sociology of Education,* vol. 41, no. 2, pp. 156–177, Spring 1968.

Bloland, Harland G.: *Higher Education Associations in a Decentralized Education System,* Center for Research and Development in Higher Education, Berkeley, Calif., 1969.

Cantarow, Ellen: "The Radicalizing of a Teacher of Literature," *Change,* vol. 4, no. 4, pp. 50–61, May 1972.

Cheit, Earl F.: *The New Depression in Higher Education: A Study of Financial Conditions at 41 Colleges and Universities,* McGraw-Hill Book Company, New York, 1971.

Colfax, J. David, and Jack L. Roach (eds.): *Radical Sociology,* Basic Books, Inc., Publishers, New York, 1971.

Dixon, Marlene: "Academic Roles and Functions," *The Insurgent Sociologist,* vol. 2, no. 2, pp. 8–17, Spring 1972.

Easton, David: "The New Revolution in Political Science," *American Political Science Review,* vol. 63, no. 4, pp. 1051–1061, December 1969.

Fisher, John Hurt: "The Modern Language Association of America, 1883–1968," *ACLS Newsletter,* vol. 20, no. 2, pp. 19–25, March 1969.

Flacks, Richard: "Towards a Socialist Sociology: Some Proposals for Work in the Coming Period," *The Insurgent Sociologist,* vol. 2, no. 2, pp. 18–27, Spring 1972.

Garbarino, Joseph W.: "Faculty Unionism: From Theory to Practice," *Industrial Relations*, vol. 11, no. 1, pp. 1–17, February 1972.

Gilb, Corinne Lathrop: *Hidden Hierarchies*, Harper & Row Publishers, Incorporated, New York, 1966.

Green, Philip, and Sanford Levinson (eds.): *Power and Community: Dissenting Essays in Political Science*, Random House, Inc., New York, 1970.

Greenberg, Daniel: "Why Politicians Don't Listen to Scientists Anymore," *Columbia Forum*, vol. 13, no. 4, pp. 14–17, Winter 1970.

Grumbach, Doris: "What Matters to the MLA," *The New Republic*, pp. 21–23, Jan. 6 and 13, 1973.

Horowitz, Irving Louis: *Professing Sociology*, Aldine Publishing Company, Chicago, 1968.

Howe, Irving: "Literary Criticism and Literary Radicals," *The American Scholar*, vol. 41, no. 1, pp. 113–120, Winter 1971–72.

Hughes, Everett Cherington: *Men and Their Work*, The Free Press of Glencoe, Inc., New York, 1958.

Jencks, Christopher, and David Riesman: *The Academic Revolution*, Doubleday & Company, Inc., Garden City, N.Y., 1968.

Kampf, Louis: "The Trouble with Literature . . . ," *Change*, vol. 2, no. 3, pp. 27–34, May–June 1970.

Kampf, Louis, and Paul Lauter (eds.): *The Politics of Literature*, Random House, Inc., New York, 1970.

Kettler, David: "The Vocation of Radical Intellectuals," *Politics and Society*, vol. 1, no. 1, pp. 23–49, November 1970.

Kiger, Joseph C.: *American Learned Societies*, Public Affairs Press, Washington, D.C., 1963.

Krause, Charles A.: "What's Left of the New Left?" *The New Republic*, pp. 17–18, Mar. 20, 1971.

Ladd, Everett, Jr., and Seymour Martin Lipset: *Professors, Unions, and American Higher Education*, Carnegie Commission on Higher Education, Berkeley, Calif., 1973.

Lane, Robert E.: "APSA Presidential Address: To Nurture a Discipline," *American Political Science Review*, vol. 66, no. 1, pp. 164–182, March 1972.

La Rue, Linda: "The Black Movement and Women's Liberation," *The Black Scholar*, vol. 1, no. 7, pp. 36–42, May 1970.

London, Herbert: "The Relevance of 'Irrelevance': History as a Functional Discipline," *New York University Education Quarterly,* vol. 2, no. 3, pp. 9–15, Spring 1971.

Lowi, Theodore J.: "Who *Should* Govern," *P.S.,* vol. 2, no. 3, pp. 276–277, Summer 1969.

Lynd, Staughton: *Restructuring the University,* New University Conference, Chicago, Ill., 1970.

Lynd, Staughton: "Prospects for the New Left," *Liberation,* vol. 15, no. 10, pp. 13–28, January 1971.

Mack, Maynard: "To See It Feelingly," *PMLA,* vol. 86, no. 3, pp. 363–374, May 1971.

Ohmann, Richard: "The MLA and the Politics of Inadvertence," *PMLA,* vol. 83, no. 4, pt. 1, pp. 988–990, September 1968*a.*

Ohmann, Richard: *Politics and Professional Organizations: A Radical View,* distributed by the Modern Language Caucus of the New University Conference, 1968*b.*

Oltman, Ruth M.: "Women in the Professional Caucuses," *American Behavioral Scientist,* vol. 15, no. 2, pp. 281–299, November–December 1971.

Orlans, Harold: *Contracting for Knowledge,* Jossey-Bass Publishers, Inc., San Francisco, 1973.

Reese, K. M.: "Scientific Societies and Public Affairs," *Chemical and Engineering News,* pp. 30–35, May 3, 1971.

Rose, Arnold: "Voluntary Associations Under Conditions of Competition and Conflict," *Social Forces,* vol. 34, no. 2, pp. 159–163, December 1955.

Roszak, Theodore (ed.): *The Dissenting Academy,* Random House, Inc., New York, 1968.

Schorske, Carl E.: "Professional Ethos and Public Crisis: A Historian's Reflections," *PMLA,* vol. 83, no. 4, pt. 1, pp. 979–984, September 1968.

Scully, Malcolm G.: "Modern Language, History Associations Weigh Question of Political Involvement," *The Chronicle of Higher Education,* vol. 3, no. 9, p. 5, Jan. 13, 1969.

Shor, Ira: "Notes on Marxism and Method," *College English,* vol. 34, no. 2, pp. 173–177, November 1972.

Sills, David: "Voluntary Associations: Instruments and Objects of Change," *Human Organization,* vol. 18, no. 1, pp. 17–21, Spring 1959.

Sjoberg, Gideon (ed.): *Ethics, Politics, and Social Research,* Schenkman Publishing Co., Inc., Cambridge, Mass., 1967.

Somit, Albert, and Joseph Tanenhaus: *American Political Science: A Profile of a Discipline*, Atherton Press, Inc., New York, 1964.

Somit, Albert, and Joseph Tanenhaus: *The Development of American Political Science: From Burgess to Behavioralism*, Allyn and Bacon, Inc., Boston, 1967.

Surkin, Marvin, and Alan Wolfe: "The Political Dimension of American Political Science," *Acta Politica*, vol. 5, no. 1, pp. 43–61, October 1969.

Surkin, Marvin, and Alan Wolfe (eds.): *An End to Political Science: The Caucus Papers*, Basic Books, Inc., Publishers, New York, 1970.

Teodori, Massimo (ed.): *The New Left: A Documentary History*, The Bobbs-Merrill Company, Inc., Indianapolis, 1969.

Unger, Irwin: "The 'New Left' and American History: Some Recent Trends in United States Historiography," *American Historical Review*, vol. 72, no. 4, pp. 1237–1263, July 1967.

Voss, John, and Paul L. Ward (eds.): *Confrontation and Learned Societies*, New York University Press, New York, 1970.

Wallerstein, Immanuel, and Paul Starr (eds.): *The University Crisis Reader*, vols. 1 and 2, Random House, Inc., New York, 1971.

Walsh, John: "American Physical Society," *Science*, vol. 180, no. 4086, pp. 576–577, May 11, 1973.

Wasson, Richard: "New Marxist Criticism: Introduction," *College English*, vol. 34, no. 2, pp. 169–172, November 1972.

Wellek, René: "The Attack on Literature," *The American Scholar*, vol. 42, no. 1, pp. 27–42, Winter 1972–73.

Wolfe, Alan: "Unthinking about the Thinkable: Reflections on the Failure of the Caucus for a New Political Science," *Politics and Society*, vol. 1, no. 3, pp. 393–406, May 1971.

Wolfle, Dael, and Charles V. Kidd: "The Future Market for Ph.D.'s," *AAUP Bulletin*, vol. 58, no. 1, pp. 5–16, Spring 1972.

Zuckerman, Harriet: "Stratification in American Science, " *Sociological Inquiry*, vol. 40, no. 2, pp. 235–257, Spring 1970.

Zuckerman, Harriet, and Robert Merton: "Sociology of Refereeing," *Physics Today*, vol. 24, no. 7, pp. 28–33, July 1971.

Appendix A: List of Persons Interviewed

Luis Alvarez, University of California, Berkeley

Sandra Bogner, New York University

Pierre Boulle, McGill University

Earl Callen, American University

Emily Card, University of California, Irvine

Owen Chamberlain, University of California, Berkeley

J. David Colfax, Washington University

Bertram Davis, American Association of University Professors

N. J. Demerath III, University of Massachusetts, Amherst

David Easton, University of Chicago

John Fairbank, Harvard University

John Hurt Fisher, University of Tennessee, Knoxville

John Hope Franklin, University of Chicago

William W. Havens, Jr., Columbia University

Tom Hecht, New University Conference

Gerald Holton, Harvard University

Judson James, City College, City University of New York

Morris Janowitz, University of Chicago

David Kettler, Trent University

Lauriston King, National Science Foundation

Mae King, American Political Science Association

Evron Kirkpatrick, American Political Science Association

Robert Lane, Yale University

Edgar Litt, University of Connecticut

Theodore Lowi, Cornell University

Edward Malecki, California State College at Los Angeles

Philip H. Malenson, Southeastern Massachusetts University

Carlos Munoz, University of California, Irvine

Carol Ohmann, Wesleyan University

Richard Ohmann, Wesleyan University

Harold Orlans, Brookings Institution

Charles Ornelas, University of California, Santa Barbara

Martin Perl, Stanford University

Philip Pitruzzello, New York University

Don K. Price, Harvard University

Edward Purcell, Harvard University

Mark Roelofs, New York University

David Riesman, Harvard University

Brian Schwartz, Massachusetts Institute of Technology

Charles Schwartz, University of California, Berkeley

James Settle, American Council of Learned Societies

Joe Shapiro, Fordham University

Irwin Sperber, University of California, Berkeley

Marvin Surkin, Adelphi University

Stanley Swart, Northwestern University

Donald Tacheron, American Political Science Association

Francis Lee Utley, Ohio State University

John Voss, American Academy of Arts and Sciences

Howard Wachtel, American University

Paul Ward, American Historical Association

Michael Walzer, Harvard University

Aaron Wildavsky, University of California, Berkeley

Alan Wolfe, Richmond College, City University of New York

Index

.